GUEST

Sign Here: ______________________________

When you sign your name on this title page, you become our partner, co-creator, and co-author in shaping your transformative journey toward your ultimate potential. Your new life begins today, as you harness the awesome power of I Am.

My coauthor, Ken Shelton, and I invite you to discover the magical power, the profound symbolism, and the extraordinary potential embedded within the I Am affirmations that impact our external conditions and our inner essence. You are about to embark on a transformative journey that will propel your personal development trajectory. As the great poet Hafiz wrote: "The words we use become the house we live in." Our reality manifests through our words.

We provide examples, personal stories, and scriptures to illustrate how I Am affirmations can help us overcome challenges and setbacks. As you ponder and apply the affirmations to your daily living and language, you will experience a paradigm shift—a new perspective on life and personal leadership. You will begin to receive better results, improved relationships, and greater self-esteem, self-worth, and net worth. You will start to heal your mind, body, and spirit.

Your inner voice, self-talk, or internal dialogue will empower you as never before on your personal odyssey. By the final pages, you will better understand the power of words. Sports legends, business moguls, spiritual leaders, and individuals in all walks of life know that every cell in our bodies is influenced by the words we think and speak. Start using affirmations today.

WHAT OTHERS ARE SAYING ABOUT DAN MCCORMICK, KEN SHELTON, AND THIS BOOK

"My father often talked of making 'deposits' in the 'emotional bank accounts' of people as a way to build trust and gain influence. In this fascinating book, Dan and Ken invite us to apply that concept to ourselves by making deposits of daily positive affirmations in our minds and in our hearts."

— Stephen M. R. Covey
Bestselling Author of *The Speed of Trust* and *Trust & Inspire*

"Is there anything left unwritten on how to be more happy, healthy, and wealthy? Dan and Ken answer that question with profound insights based on the biblical concept of *I Am*. They present a construct that will surely change the life of anyone who is truly seeking a healthier, happier, more productive and positive path."

— Truman Hunt
Former CEO of Nu Skin Enterprises, Inc.

"This wonderful book makes a great gift for all the people we love. When we read the *I Am* affirmations, we may question our ability to live such lofty aspirations; however, when we commit fully to being present and living in the state of *I Am*, we are assisted by a Higher Power. Combining faith, effort, and commitment, we can all achieve the *I Am* affirmations; and I promise: as we do, our lives are richly blessed. Our success is multiplied, and our self-confidence skyrockets when we do what we promise ourselves daily."

— Jason Hewlett
CSP, CPAE, Hall of Fame Speaker, Award-Winning Entertainer, and Author of *The Promise to the One*

"Are you ready to elevate your attitude and brighten your outlook on the world? In *Awakening Who I Am*, Dan McCormick and Ken Shelton provide you the guiding light and step-by-step process to create your own "I Am" positive and powerful affirmations. Follow their guidance, and you will greet each day knowing you can make a positive impact on the world."

— Sharon Lechter
New York Times Bestselling Author, Co-Author of
Rich Dad Poor Dad and fourteen other Rich Dad books,
Outwitting the Devil, *Three Feet from Gold*, and Author of
Think and Grow Rich for Women

"Repeat after me, 'I Am Capable. I Am Worthy. I Am a Creator.' Dan McCormick and Ken Shelton will have you believing these and many more affirmations about yourself after you read this book. Best of all, all of those things are true, and you will begin to believe and embody them. When you adopt these positive affirmations, you will begin to take charge of creating your own destiny, and what a wonderful journey it will be."

— Patrick Snow
Publishing Coach and International Bestselling Author of
Creating Your Own Destiny and *The Affluent Entrepreneur*

"In *Awakening Who I Am*, you will experience a jolt of positivity to your brain that will have you eager to face each day believing you are capable of achieving anything you set your mind to. Dan McCormick and Ken Shelton will teach you seven powerful affirmations—one for each day of the week—that will change your thoughts and change your world. *I Am* excited for you."

— Tyler R. Tichelaar, PhD
Award-Winning Author of
Narrow Lives and *Kawbawgam: The Chief, The Legend, The Man*

"Awakening Who I Am by Dan McCormick and Ken Shelton is a transformative exploration into the essence of self-identity and the boundless potential that unfolds when we discover our true selves. Dan and Ken masterfully guide readers on a journey of self-discovery, illuminating the path to uncovering our authentic identities with wisdom, empathy, and actionable insights. As someone who has dedicated my life to inspiring others and pushing the boundaries of what's possible, I am profoundly moved by the depth and power of the authors' message. This book is not just a read; it's an awakening to the incredible possibilities that lie within each of us. I wholeheartedly endorse Awakening Who I Am as a vital compass for anyone seeking to understand their true identity and unlock their full potential."

— Chad Hymas
Best-Selling Author and World-Renowned Speaker

"I met Dan more than twenty years ago when a mutual friend told me he was a huge Og Mandino fan. That began a friendship that continues to this day. I have been up close and personal observing Dan's journey. Awakening Who I Am is not just a book. This is a lifetime of preparation through very difficult and challenging trials and extraordinary wins. This is the essence of the man and the foundation of who Dan is. Feast on these words knowing it is possible to experience the same awakening for yourself. Thank you, Dan and Ken, for being the example of these principles and for the treasure of this book!"

— Dave Blanchard
Bestselling Author of *Today I Begin a New Life*,
CEO, The Og Mandino Companies

"Are you ready? If you're reading this book, you're already a high achiever—or want to be. Are you ready to take your personal and professional performance to the next level? Dan and Ken share success stories and provide a clear blueprint that will support you in reaching next level performance. Morning by morning. Day by day. Week by week. Year by year. Are you ready?"

— Daniel Rex
Chief Executive Officer, Toastmasters International

"What I liked most about *Awakening Who I Am* is the way in which the authors work to demystify I Am statements. By intentionally selecting seven specific I Am statements, they carefully detail how each of the statements can play out in your own life through interesting stories and examples. The book showcases their deep knowledge of I Am and is ideal for anyone who wants to use this powerful tool."

— Andrea Waltz
Co-Author, *Go for No!*

"Dan and Ken breathe life and positivity into this book. The message about how you define yourself is very clear and very core. *Awakening Who I Am* is the right book at the right time."

— Dr. Benjamin Hardy
Best-Selling Author of *Be Your Future Self Now*

7 KEY AFFIRMATIONS TO EMPOWER YOUR LIFE

AWAKENING WHO "I AM"

TWO WORDS TO IGNITE YOUR TRANSFORMATION

DAN McCORMICK
KEN SHELTON

FOREWORD BY HAL ELROD
AFTERWORD BY DR. BENJAMIN HARDY

AWAKENING WHO *I AM*
Two Words to Ignite Your Transformation

For additional copies/bulk purchases of this book, please contact:
Dan@AffirmIAm.com

Paperback ISBN: 979-8-9914727-1-5
Hard Cover ISBN: 979-8-9914727-2-2

For more information on supporting content, speeches, and related products or services see www.AffirmIAm.com.

Cover Designer: Fusion Creative Works

Every attempt has been made to properly source all quotes.

Printed in the United States of America.

First Edition

2 4 6 8 10 12

DEDICATION

We dedicate this book to all courageous creators, authors, innovators, entrepreneurs, and finishers; and to the many uncommon men and women who overcome opposition to lead great lives and to bless others.

In a sense, this book is a tribute to the many remarkable people we have met and a distillation of affirmations we have learned from them. We do not claim to be the world's most amazing entrepreneurs or greatest salesmen, but we do claim to be partnered with those who truly are the "greatest generation" of entrepreneurs the world has ever known.

ACKNOWLEDGMENTS

We gratefully acknowledge several people for their influence on our life and our work.

Dan: I Am blessed to associate with so many people who influence my thinking and inspire me to be the best husband, father, friend, speaker, and coach I can be.

Patricia Acosta • Margie Aliprandi • Jerry and Jan Anderson
McKenzie Anderson • Dr. Luis Arriaza
Patrick and Tracey Baum • Crystal Beazer • Bob Beaudine
Jay Bennett • Scott Bennett • Ty Bennett • Ty Best • Paige Bischoff
Dave Blanchard • Paul Blanchard • Chelsea Boyes • Kenny Brady
Sean and Cherrie Brady • Cara Brooks • Sue and Bob Burdick
Bob Burg • Christiana Burrton • Simon Chan • Adrian Chenault
Tom Chenault • Xander Clark • Lance Conrad • Mindy Deeble
Danelle Delgado • Ed Deritter • Gary Deritter • Amanda Earnest
Fred Elias • Lisa Faeder Grossman • Rebecca Fahr • Todd Falcone
John Haramza • Jason and Vanessa Harris • Nigel Henry
Roz Hobbs • Robert Hollis • Cheryl Huffman • Donna Johnson
Rick Jordan • Julia Keeton • Thomas Kogler
Peggy Anderson Krock • Sharon Lechter • Stephen McNeal
Susie Mollison • Greg Montoya • Dr. Stephen Moore
Alan Nagao • Charley Patterson • Justin Prince

Wen Rosencrance • Nathan Ricks • Paige and Laird Riffle
Johnn Soleder • Todd Speciale • Ditrius Siruno
Deanne and Mark Stidham • Larry and Taylor Thompson
Troy Thompson • Dr. Bill and Julie Toth • Laurie Ulrich
Mitzi Vaughan • Alan and Pam Vickers • Ricky Villanueva
Andrea Waltz • Ben Ward • Eileen Williams • Kenton Worthington
Jeff and Dianna Zisselman

Ken: I thank Dan McCormick for being a passionate champion of entrepreneurship, sales, and direct marketing. I acknowledge the valuable mentorship of my late friend Stephen R. Covey and all the thought leaders who contributed to our Leadership Excellence magazines and books for the thirty years I served as editor and publisher. And I thank my wife and family for their unconditional love and support.

CONTENTS

FOREWORD

By Hal Elrod

Knowing Dan as I do, I cannot think of anyone better suited or with a more timely approach to help you to better your life. Ken Shelton and Dan McCormick most certainly have created in *Awakening Who I Am* the information and tools you need to make the positive, self-affirming changes you desire. Let me explain to you why I wholeheartedly believe that.

AFFIRM YOUR MIRACLE

Growing up, I was fairly mediocre at just about everything I did. I didn't get good grades in school, wasn't an athlete, nor was I popular.

At age fifteen, I got lucky and ended up as a radio DJ with my own weekly show. That was a dream come true for me. Then at nineteen, one of my closest friends talked me into temporarily putting my dream on hold to work for a direct marketing company, Cutco Cutlery. Although I lacked confidence in myself, I borrowed confidence from my mentor and went on to become one of the top salespeople in the company's history.

Then, in 2008, everything changed. When I was at the lowest point in my life—a failing business, drowning in debt, deeply depressed, and in the worst physical shape of my life—I started using affirmation and visualization as part of a daily personal development ritual I called my Miracle Morning—I called it that because it transformed my life so fast that it felt like a miracle. I was able to build successful businesses, more than double my income, become a keynote speaker, pay off my debts, and complete a fifty-two-mile ultra-marathon in less than twelve months!

I can now affirm a universal truth—*I Am* worthy, deserving, and capable of achieving what I want in life.

You, too, can significantly increase your ability to earn and attract better health and more monetary wealth by making daily affirmations and visualizing a part of your daily life until they become your new normal. Then, you can stop settling for less than you truly desire and deserve and start living in alignment with your vision of the most extraordinary life you can imagine.

You might affirm: *I Am* becoming the best version of myself. The new me. Who you are becoming is the single most important determining factor in your quality of life—something I learned the hard way by experiencing three painful wake-up calls.

WAKE-UP CALL 1: FOUND DEAD AT THE SCENE

On December 3, 1999, I received my first standing ovation after giving a speech to my colleagues. I felt on top of the world, but while driving home my Ford Mustang, I was hit head-on by a drunk driver at more than seventy miles per hour. My car was propelled into oncoming traffic, where another vehicle crashed into my driver's side door.

In the crash, I broke eleven bones, suffered permanent brain damage, and lost much blood. One hour later, I was removed from the wreckage and found dead at the scene. I had quit breathing, and my heart had stopped beating for six minutes! Six days later, when I woke up from a coma, my doctors told me I would likely never walk again. But harnessing the power of unwavering faith (in God, in myself, and in the mind's ability to heal the body), I took my first step three weeks later.

WAKE-UP CALL 2: MIRACLE MORNING IS BORN

In 2007, the US economy crashed, and like millions of Americans, I crashed with it. I lost half of my income, racked up $52,000 in credit card debt, and my home was foreclosed on by the bank. I felt hopeless. I became depressed. I was desperate. Desperation turned into inspiration to develop and do a daily personal development ritual so I could start becoming the person I needed to be. I woke up the next morning and started my day with six timeless growth practices (life SAVERS)—**S**ilence, **A**ffirmations, **V**isualization, **E**xercise, **R**eading, and **S**cribing), and within two months, I had more than doubled my income, trained for a fifty-two-mile ultra-marathon, and started writing *The Miracle Morning* book.

WAKE-UP CALL 3: A 20-30 PERCENT CHANCE OF SURVIVING CANCER

At age thirty-seven, I nearly died again when my heart, lungs, and kidneys were on the verge of failing. After seven visits to the ER to have my lung drained, and opinions from three hospitals, I was diagnosed with a rare, aggressive form of cancer: Acute Lymphoblastic Leukemia (ALL). Doctors told me I had a 20-30 percent chance of surviving. As a father with a seven-year-old daughter and a four-year-old son, that was about the worst news I could have received. However, I could choose how I would respond, and my chosen response was to be the happiest and most grateful person while I endured the most difficult time in my life because in my mind, there was a 100 percent chance I would survive.

PLEASE KNOW THIS: NO MATTER HOW BAD LIFE GETS, THERE IS ALWAYS A WAY TO TURN IT AROUND.

My way was Miracle Morning. I committed to making time—one hour in the early morning—for my daily personal development. I was not a "morning person," but I figured if I made that first hour optimally productive, the rest of the day would fall into place. I started waking up at 5 a.m. to do my personal development routine—ten minutes for six life-changing practices: meditation, affirmation, journaling, visualization, reading, and exercise. For the next few weeks, I continued to wake up at 5 a.m. and do my sixty-minute routine. I had more energy, clarity, and focus—and within sixty days, my income was higher than ever before.

If you want your life to be different, you have to do something different.

POWER OF AFFIRMATIONS

Regarding affirmations, I had never before harnessed their power. After reading the self-confidence affirmation from *Think and Grow Rich*, I decided to write my own affirmation: what I wanted, who I was committed to being, and what I was committed to doing to change my life.

I affirm: You are, or *I Am* just as worthy, deserving, and capable of creating and sustaining extraordinary health, wealth, happiness, love, and success in your life as any other person.

Start living in alignment with that truth and stop settling for less than you deserve. Dedicate time each day to becoming the person you need to be—one who is qualified and capable of consistently attracting, creating, and sustaining success.

How you start each day—your morning routine—dramatically affects your success. Focused, productive, and successful mornings generate focused, productive, and successful days, weeks, and inevitably, a successful life—faster than you ever thought possible.

One of the greatest gifts each of us can give to those we love and those we lead is to fulfill our potential because in doing so, we can help others do the same.

And that's what Dan McCormick and Ken Shelton want for us: an abundant life!

If you want to change your life, you must change what you focus on. I truly believe affirmations—when done correctly—have the power to transform our lives. Whether your goals are to achieve financial abundance, overcome fear, be happy, maximize your impact in this world, or do something else entirely, affirmations can help you make your dreams a reality.

In my book *The Miracle Equation*, I note that an affirmation is simply intentionally designed language for the purpose of directing your focus toward something you aspire to change or embody in your life—a reminder of what matters most to you, such as an important goal, a daily action, an empowering feeling, a mindset, a value, a purpose, or anything you want to keep at the forefront of your mind to stay focused on what is most important to you.

As you affirm your commitment to live every day with unwavering faith and extraordinary effort, take a deep breath, and as you inhale, feel your new identity wash over you. Think about what it would look like, sound like, and feel like. This exercise will help you experience your new identity both intellectually and emotionally. Use language that resonates with you.

Edit and update your affirmations as needed to keep up with your evolving identity and goals. I'm constantly editing and updating my affirmations as I continue to learn, grow, and gain new perspectives. We all have a lot of reprogramming to do. We have many years of limiting beliefs and internal conflicts to unravel and fears to overcome. I recommend writing affirmations for each area of your life and with each affirmation include specific goals for becoming the person you want to be. This book will show you how.

Hal Elrod

Hal Elrod
Host of *Achieve Your Goals* podcast
Best-Selling Author of *The Miracle Morning* and
The Miracle Equation

INTRODUCTION

A Note to the Reader

"Your greatest awakening comes when you are aware about your infinite nature."

— Amit Ray

Why the title...*Awakening Who I Am?*

We considered many possible titles for this book and finally arrived at *Awakening Who I Am* because from start to finish, we invite you to address the question: Who am I?

- Am I who I say *I Am*?
- Am I who I affirm *I Am*?
- Am I who I see reflected in the mirror?
- Am I who others in authority tell me *I Am*?
- Am I who I think, behave, act, or perform as?

Is my core identity based in theology, ideology, biology, physiology, or psychology?

Can I be anything or anybody I want or choose to be? Yes, within certain parameters. However, you cannot change your core identity, regardless of your theology or ideology.

Can I transition, transform, even transgender, and affirm it in iambic pentameter? Yes, you can make major transitions and write all about it. However, you might bend so far in redefining yourself that you break your original wellness and wholeness.

To arrive at the best answer to the question *Who Am I?*, you may need to awaken who you are, truly and authentically.

What is an awakening? Awakening literally means waking from sleep or slumber; however, an awakening might figuratively mean…

- rousing from inactivity or indifference
- reviving interest in something
- coming into existence or awareness
- suddenly becoming aware of something

You and I may have one or more awakening experiences. Some can be crude and rude while others inspirational and transformational. These experiences tend to last only a few seconds or minutes, seldom more than an hour, but they can have a life-changing impact.

> *"You are one thing only. You are a Divine Being, an all-powerful Creator. You are a Deity in jeans and a t-shirt, and within you dwells the infinite wisdom of the ages and the sacred creative force of All that is, will be and ever was."*
>
> — Anthon St. Maarten

As Steve Taylor, PhD, suggests: Awakening expands our awareness and intensifies our feelings. We transcend the thoughts that normally preoccupy us and feel a sense of elation or serenity. Our perceptions become more vivid, and we sense a keen connection to nature and to other people, a sense of love and compassion, a sense that we have ascended beyond our limited self-identity and become more authentic, at one with the universe, resulting in a major change in paradigm, perspective, or values and delivering a greater sense of trust, confidence, hope, peace, and optimism.

We become more positive and resilient; we are better able to cope with hardship. We express gratitude for the good people and things in our life. Awakenings often lead to lifestyle changes, new interests, new relationships, new careers, and new sources of income.

"A kind of light spread out from her. And everything changed color. And the world opened out. And a day was good to awaken to. And there were no limits to anything. And the people of the world were good and handsome. And I was not afraid anymore."

— John Steinbeck

"She remembered who she was…and the game changed."

— Lalah Delia

Awakening experiences have a powerful therapeutic or healing effect and shift your consciousness and awareness. While you may experience a sudden, dramatic, and seemingly irreversible awakening, you are most likely to go through a process in which new consciousness gradually flows into and transforms everything you are and do.

Thinking becomes the servant of presence or awareness—conscious connection with universal intelligence. Awakening may happen when you become aware of the thoughts you habitually think, especially your persistent negative thoughts—the critical self-talk you have been identified with all your life.

"When one realizes one is asleep, at that moment one is already half-awake."

— P. D. Ouspensky

"Your own Self-Realization is the greatest service you can render the world."

— Ramana Maharshi

Affirming who you are facilitates awakening who you are. When you awaken who you are, your authentic self, you gain awareness and presence. You can then make a conscious choice to be present rather than to be absent and indulge in useless and wasteful thinking. You invite presence and peace into your life. Once awakened, your motives and motivations change. You open yourself up to an emerging consciousness and start bringing its light into your life, your relationships, your work, and your world. Once awakened, you stop waiting for something significant to happen in your life and start making it happen.

Ken Shelton

SECTION I

WIN WITH AFFIRMATIONS

— CHAPTER 1 —

WHY AFFIRMATIONS?

"Affirmations to me are the most misunderstood and the most effective form of personal development."

— Hal Elrod

CREED OF THE UNCOMMON MAN

I do not choose to be a common man. It is my right to be uncommon—if I can. I seek opportunity not security. I do not wish to be a kept citizen, humbled and dulled by having the state look after me. I want to take the calculated risk; to dream and to build, to fail and to succeed. I refuse to barter incentive for a dole. I prefer the challenges of life to the guaranteed existence; the thrill of fulfillment to the stale calm of utopia. I will not trade freedom for beneficence nor my dignity for a handout. I will never cower before any master nor bend to any threat. It is my heritage to stand erect, proud and unafraid; to think and act for myself, enjoy the benefit of my creations and to face the world boldly and say, "This I have done."

— Dean Alfange, American Statesman

What do you call yourself or tell yourself when you talk to yourself (self-talk)? Do you use affirmations or defamations?

If you were to record and play back all the things you say to yourself in a day, you might be amazed at the degree of negativity, and you might then say in disbelief and denial (along with former New York Yankee catcher Yogi Berra):

"I really didn't *say* everything I said."

Or at least, "I really didn't *mean* everything I said."

If that's the case, then why say it in the first place, especially if it's only going to confuse you...or confine you in old mental ruts and physical routines?

Martial artist and actor Bruce Lee once said, "Don't speak negatively about yourself, even as a joke. Your body doesn't know the difference. Words are energy and cast spells. Change the way you speak about yourself, and you can change your life. What you're not changing, you're also choosing."

The good news is this: "It ain't over till it's over."

LIFE AND TIME TO MAKE AFFIRMATIONS

If you are reading this, you must still have *life*, and that means you still have *time*—time to change the narrative and the conditions of your life; time to affirm your worth.

And you can start by affirming, "*I Am*...a winner or *I Am* a miracle." As a quote popularly attributed to Einsteins says, "There are only two ways to live your life. One is as though nothing is a miracle. The other is as though everything is a miracle."

When you make affirmations, you join an elite club of superachievers who live their lives as if everything is a miracle.

Ali's Case in Point: We all recall Muhammad Ali constantly affirming, "*I Am* the greatest"—and he became the greatest heavyweight boxer of his time.

Vidmar's Case in Point: When Peter Vidmar was performing as a gymnast at UCLA and hoping to make the US Olympic team, he would visualize being in the Olympics, competing against China, doing a perfect routine, and winning the gold medal. On July 31, 1984, Peter was actually there, and his coach affirmed: "You are prepared. You know what to do. You've done it a thousand times. Just do it one more time." Peter did it one more time to win a gold medal.

Peter says: "We can all benefit by setting goals, visualizing them, affirming them by asking, 'How will I feel when I achieve this goal?' and letting that feeling guide us."

Carrey's Case in Point: In 1985, while struggling to find work and often sleeping in his car, Jim Carrey wrote himself a $10 million check for "acting services rendered," dated it ten years in the future, and kept it in his wallet. In 1995, Carrey was cast in *Dumb and Dumber* for $10 million. Jim later buried the check with his father, who often drove his son to appear at comedy clubs.

Carrey's story illustrates the power of the Law of Attraction, of faith and belief, of visualization and affirmation, and of putting our ideas in writing.

A's Case in Point: In the summer of 2002, the Oakland A's were losing more baseball games than they were winning, after manager Billy Beane traded two all-star players in an experiment called "moneyball." On August 13, with the team at its lowest point, Beane came into the locker room before the game and gave a short speech and affirmation: "You may not look like a winning team, but you are a winning team! Now go out there and play like one."

The new-look A's, despite a comparative lack of star power, surprised the baseball world by winning the next twenty games, setting an American League record for most consecutive wins.

Likewise, you may not look like a winner today, but we affirm: You are a winner!

Now, all that remains is for you to affirm: *I Am* a winner…and then to play like one in your own experiment with gold medals, millions of dollars, moneyballs, or miracle mornings.

When I, Dan, first watched the documentary *Miracle Morning*, I heard Hal Elrod speak about the experiment he calls Miracle Morning, and about the amazing difference his new morning routine made in his life. I sat up straight in my chair and committed then and there to try it. Each morning, I had a new intentionality for the day. With a strong desire to experience the many benefits mentioned by Hal, I started my sixty-minute routine at 5 a.m. the very next day, and I have continued almost every morning since then. I can now affirm: *I Am* the morning miracle!

In her book *The Game of Life*, Florence Scovel Shinn tells us how to win: "Invisible forces are ever working, though we do not know it. Owing to the vibratory power of words, whatever we voice, we begin to attract." Voicing affirmations attracts and invites miracles.

And in his book *Power Versus Force*, David R. Hawkins writes: "The reciprocal of René Descartes' famous phrase 'I think, therefore *I Am*' is '*I Am*; therefore, I think.' *I Am* is a statement of awareness, witnessing that the capacity for experience is independent of form."

UNIVERSAL APPLICATION OF AFFIRMATIONS

Today, affirmations are often associated with modern self-help, personal development, positive thinking, and self-improvement, but their origins trace to ancient times. Affirmations have a long and rich history, rooted in ancient spiritual practices and traditions, including Hinduism, Buddhism, Stoicism, and Christianity.

- In Hinduism, the practice of repeating a sacred word or mantra (known as *japa*) invites a sense of calm and inner peace.
- Similarly, Buddhist monks use chanting as a meditation practice to calm the mind and invite the spirit. *Om* or *Aum*, the Sanskrit mantra often chanted in yoga sessions, is said to be the sound of the creation, representing the divinity and enlightenment within us.
- The Stoics, ancient Greek philosophers, believed in positive self-talk and the power of affirmations. They encouraged their followers to repeat stoic mantras that focused on virtues such as courage, wisdom, and self-control.
- In the Bible, we read of Christ making several *I Am* affirmations of his identity.

Modern personal affirmations may be traced to French psychologist Emile Coué (1857–1926) who developed autosuggestion—affirming positive statements repeatedly in order to achieve a desired outcome. He noted: "If we truly believe in our affirmations, we could overcome our limitations and achieve greater personal empowerment."

Today, affirmations are widely used by individuals from all walks of life as an empowering way to overcome limiting beliefs and self-defeating behaviors and increase positivity and productivity. When practiced consistently, affirmations can help reprogram the brain, rescript the mind, and overcome negative self-talk and self-destructive addictions.

People who practice self-affirmation exercises tend to experience less stress, fear, and anxiety, perhaps because affirmations help us gain a greater sense of autonomy or self-governance—leading life according to our values and authentic desires. By repeating positive statements regularly, we shift our focus toward what we want to achieve and set positive intentions, which increases our motivation and drive to set and accomplish goals.

By applying the Seven Affirmations, we can overcome negative self-talk and limiting beliefs, reprogram our mindset, and cultivate well-being, success, inner peace, health, and wealth.

WHY SEVEN AFFIRMATIONS?

The number 7 is the number of perfection, security, safety, and rest. As an early prime number in the series of positive integers, the number 7 has many symbolic associations in religion, mythology, superstition, and philosophy. Here are just a few examples:

- There are 7 days in a week and 7 colors in the rainbow.
- 7 circles form the symbol "The Seed of Life," symbolizing the six days of creation and the central circle symbolizes the day of rest.
- The number 7 is often considered lucky and especially lucky for Cancer and Pisces.
- There are 7 notes to the diatonic scale.
- There are 7 letters in the Roman numeral system.
- Number 7 is the number of Neptune.

- In the Tarot, 7 is the card of the Chariot, symbolic of the need to focus. Reversed, it signifies the inability to see things through and finish what we start.
- The opposite sides of a dice always equal the number 7 when added.
- In Japan, there are 7 Lucky Gods who have a Treasure Ship; they arrive in town every New Year and give gifts to all worthy people.
- In Japan, the Festival of 7 Herbs is celebrated on January 7 every year. The Japanese eat a 7-herb rice porridge for good health and longevity.
- In Hindu weddings, the bride and groom walk around the holy fire 7 times during the ceremony, take 7 steps together, and say a vow for each step.
- There are 7 Wonders of the Ancient World, 7 Liberal Arts, and the 7 Hills of Rome.
- There are 7 Gifts of the Holy Spirit, as defined by Saint Thomas Aquinas, 7 sacraments in the Catholic Church, and 7 Deadly Sins.
- In the Bible, 7 is mentioned many times. For example, on the 7th day God finished his work and rested; 7 priests with 7 trumpets walked around the city of Jericho 7 times on the 7th day.
- In *The Book of Revelation*, we read of 7 Stars, 7 Golden Lamp Stands, 7 Spirits who had 7 bowls of wrath, and 7 plagues, 7 thunders, 7 seals, 7 angels, and 7 trumpets.
- In Judaism, we see the 7-branched Candelabrum. The Menorah has been a symbol for about 3,000 years, a reminder to be a light to all nations, a symbol of the burning bush seen by Moses, and a symbol of the 7 days of creation.

- In Islam, there are 7 verses in the first *sura* (chapter) in the Qur'an.
- During the pilgrimage to Mecca, pilgrims walk around the Kaaba 7 times.
- There are 7 Heavens in Islam and 7 Gates of Hell

Suffice it to say, the number 7 has many meanings and applications.

OUR AIM IN MAKING AFFIRMATIONS

In this book, our aim is to deliver on the big promise that we can win the week and achieve whole health and wealth—a concept that is much more inclusive than fitness and money—by following the prescribed pattern of daily affirmations, week after week.

It's a positive, purpose-driven, principle-centered, people-oriented, and practice-disciplined approach to health, wealth, and fulfillment. And it leads us to find or create the right work for us—a way of making a living that uses natural talents and nurtured levers for leverage.

In effect, like Moses, we want to help deliver people from bondage and lead them beyond the Red Sea (of debt) and the wilderness (of scarcity) into the blue ocean of abundance, to a land flowing with milk and honey. And we aim to do this not in forty years but in one week!

Yes, you can start to experience whole health and wealth in one week—and over time, week after progressive week, gain real wealth and health to enjoy the fullness of life.

Whole Health and Wealth, as wrote Henry David Thoreau, is "the ability to fully experience life." The challenge is to understand what it means to "fully experience life."

Please consider this simple question: How long does it take to change the course of your life? Behavioral scientists say that it takes at least three weeks of consistent daily behavior to ingrain habits that constitute a course correction. And yet unforeseen events, like a heart attack, can change your life in a second—or a spiritual awakening, a single mental revelation, or a flash of genius or inspiration might change the course of your life in an instant!

That kind of change—a mindset change, paradigm shift, or change in how you perceive the world and your place in it—can also happen in a flash. But we give you more time than one day—we invite you to invest one week of your time with us. In return, we promise to provide you with a pattern that, if followed faithfully, will enable you to create and sustain whole health and wealth for yourself and others, day after day, week after week, for the rest of your life. Naturally, whole wealth includes whole health—since if you ruin your health in pursuit of wealth, you'll spend your wealth trying to regain your health and happiness.

Please accept our invitation and experience ongoing progress that propels you from here (your current condition) to there (desired future state), beyond mythology and ideology to the wisdom of health and wealth in harmony with natural laws and principles.

The ancients had this right: natural laws preside over and govern the earth and all things on the face of the earth. Similarly, there are natural laws and principles (what we call Universal Principles or UPs) that ultimately govern our lives—and have the power to lift us up as we live in harmony with them or drag us down as we ignore or disobey them.

In essence, we are applying the study (science) and theology (conscience) of *I Am* affirmations. By theology, we're not taking about religion. Rather, we're referring to the all-inclusive truth of all wisdom traditions and all arts and sciences—in fact, the very fountain from which they emanate, all other sciences being branches growing out of this one taproot. All works of good conscience originate from this all-encompassing science and conscience.

As we travel the world, we find truth in all traditions and cultures. In the big picture, faith (in some unseen but incontrovertible reality) is ultimately what this book is about. And in prodding you to take a leap of faith, we seek to strike at the root of all woe.

Henry David Thoreau noted: "For every thousand hacking at the leaves of evil, there is one striking at the root." We believe the temporal fruits of health, wealth, and happiness emanate from the spiritual roots.

From our experience, we know this: Faith makes the fountain flow. If ever there was a truism, that's it. And what is true for one is true for all, including you, whoever you are.

SPIRIT OF *I AM*: *I* (EXIST) *AM* (WITH GOD)

Spirit is the best and surest source of positive energy. Spirit can come into the lives of all those who seek and prepare themselves to receive it, and we invite Spirit as we make positive affirmations. We agree with what Parley P. Pratt wrote in *Key to the Science of Theology*:

> You possess every organ, attribute, sense, sympathy, affection, of will, wisdom, love, power and gift possessed by God—except that in you these attributes are in embryo and are to be gradually developed. They resemble a bud, a seed germ, which gradually develops into bloom, and then, by progress, produces the mature fruit after its own kind. The gift of the Holy Spirit adapts to all these organs or attributes. It quickens

> all the intellectual faculties, increases, enlarges, expands and purifies all natural passions and affections, and adapts them, by the gift of wisdom, to their lawful use. It inspires, develops, cultivates and matures all the fine-toned sympathies, joys, tastes, kindred feelings and affections of our nature. It inspires virtue, kindness, goodness, tenderness, gentleness and charity. It develops beauty of person, form and features. It tends to health, vigor, animation and social feeling. It develops and invigorates all the faculties of the physical and intellectual man (and woman). It strengthens, invigorates and gives tone to the nerves. In short, it is, as it were, marrow to the bone, joy to the heart, light to the eyes, music to the ears, and life to the whole being. In the presence of such persons, one feels to enjoy the light of their countenances, as the genial rays of a sunbeam. Their very being emits a warm glow of pure gladness and sympathy, to the heart and nerves of others who have kindred feelings, or sympathy of spirit.

If we hope to gain, maintain, and sustain the spirit of positivity over time, we need to tap into the best possible sources. And the best, most sustainable and renewable source of positive energy is, in a word, spirit...generosity of spirit, brightness of spirit, lightness of spirit, warmth of spirit, and even the genius of spirit: perspective and positive affirmation.

Where can we find spirit, this prize source of positivity? We may find it in nature or nurture, in positive people, and in places and things like good books, music, dance, arts, and scripture.

Internally, we may find spirit in our heart and mind; in fact, we affirm that we may become a consistent source of spirit that others look to for light, love, laughter, and hope.

THE SCIENCE OF *I AM* AFFIRMATIONS

In making affirmations, you make the voice and vision in your imagination stronger than your current conditions. You write affirmations in first person, present tense, as if you already are that person you envision, or as if you already live in the new home, or as if you've already won the game, or as if the goal is already achieved. If you trigger the right imagery and emotion, your subconscious will believe you. You are not lying to yourself. Instead, you are simply altering your image of reality. Affirmations create powerful images and incentives for change.

You don't affirm ability or potential; rather, you affirm achievement and performance: "*I Am* a loving parent" or "*I Am* a dynamic leader."

If you don't affirm in present tense, you won't create the motivation and energy necessary to achieve desired results. You'll spin your wheels and wonder, *Why can't I change?*

The Science of Affirmations also requires that you affirm positive traits to tap into positive energy and intrinsic motivation, away from negative energy and extrinsic motivation.

You imagine "trigger images" of what you want, even if you don't have the slightest idea of how you will achieve the goal. By powerfully imprinting your goals and creating positive images of what you want and then looking at the way things are now, you create cognitive dissonance and the motivation to make the images match. When we hold inconsistent or conflicting thoughts, perceptions, beliefs, values, or attitudes, we experience mental discomfort and are intrinsically motivated to ease the tension between what we believe and how we behave, or between our vision, mission, affirmation, or goal and our current performance.

SCIENCE-BASED BENEFITS

Neuroscience and MRI evidence show that certain neural pathways in the brain are increased when we practice self-affirmation, and research in applied positive psychology confirms that using positive *I Am* affirmations delivers many potential benefits. Affirmations can:

- Reduce stress and anxiety and cultivate a sense of inner peace, optimism, positivity, and hopefulness. Promote better sleep at night to increase energy in the morning. Reinforce your positive beliefs and restructure cognitive processes.
- Enhance performance, achievement, and goal attainment in academic, athletic, and professional arenas. Adapt faster to different circumstances, roles, and situations.
- Increase resilience—the ability to cope with or bounce back from adversity, negative experiences, difficulties, social pressures, and health challenges. Make lasting, long-term changes to the ways you think and feel. Gain resilience by looking in the mirror each morning while reciting affirmations to determine how you want the day to go.
- Enhance self-image, self-esteem, self-worth, self-concept, self-integrity, self-identity, self-efficacy, self-control, and self-acceptance. We maintain self-integrity by acting in ways that authentically merit acknowledgment and praise. We use certain affirmations because we seek to deserve praise for acting in ways consistent with our personal values.
- Improve health and wellness: Positive affirmations may have a positive impact on physical, mental, and emotional health and lead to healthier habits and behaviors. For example, anxiety and depression are often associated with distorted thoughts like over-generalization and over-exaggeration of negative things. We can use affirmations to accelerate healing

and improve health; eat and drink more wisely; cease self-defeating habits; and overcome addictions.

THE HELIOTROPIC POWER OF POSITIVITY AND AFFIRMATION

Our friend Kim Cameron, an expert in Positive Psychology, often writes and speaks on the heliotropic effect, the natural tendency of all living organisms and systems to move toward life-giving and life-affirming light and away from darkness and danger.

He reports that positive affirmations and practices produce much better outcomes—better results and better relationships. And, fortunately, we naturally search for light. Many "light" metaphors frame the way we think about hope, optimism, and overcoming darkness, opposition, and challenges. We speak such phrases as "There's light at the end of the tunnel" or "You're the light of my life" or "My mind is illuminated" or "What a bright idea!" or "He's a shining example" or, even, when we're about to die, "Go toward the light."

Positive affirmations have the power to accelerate our progression; in fact, daily practice of our 7 powerful and positive *I Am* affirmations can produce a powerful heliotropic effect.

AFFIRMATION IN ACTION

1. What are your thoughts about yourself when you're not consciously thinking?

____

____

____

____

____

____

2. Of the science-based benefits you just read, which is most exciting or important for you to manifest?

____
____
____
____
____
____

SUMMARY

- You are a miracle and a winner.
- Affirmations are used around the world by cultures past and present of all backgrounds and faiths.
- Positive affirmations positively impact your physical, mental, and emotional health.
- Positive affirmations can lead to healthier habits and behaviors.
- It is the natural tendency of all life to move toward life-affirming light.

We invite you to begin using positive I Am statements. We invite you to be a co-creator of this book by sharing your unique ideas, stories, and thoughts in **your journal** as an addition to this book.

— CHAPTER 2 —

AUTHOR AND FINISHER

"Excellence is never an accident. It is always the result of high intention, sincere effort, and intelligent execution."

— Aristotle

BE PROACTIVE AND FINISH WHAT YOU START

Start reading this book—or start writing your own—with the intention to finish it and follow it. Affirm now: *I Am* an author and finisher.

Ken: When I first met Dan McCormick, he talked about affirmations and paraphrased from Hebrews 12:2: *I Am* the author and finisher....

And I wondered, *Of what might you and I be the author, creator, and finisher?*

- We might author words (letters, epistles, articles, books)
- We might author works (homes, products, and projects)
- We might author or authenticate a state of being or doing (faith, hope, charity)

We need to be wise in what we choose to author, asking: Is what *I Am* about to author worthy of my time and talent? Will it edify others? What is my primary motive? Am I seeking first to bless, not impress, seeking first the health and welfare of my audience, not my wealth?

I AM INVITATION: BE A CO-CREATOR

Again, we invite you to be a "co-creator" of this book and add your name on the title page. Yes, while reading this book, you are invited to become a contributing author by writing a chapter, by adding your unique ideas, stories, and thoughts in your journal. You will then have the option to have your book printed or added to our book in various electronic editions.

As famed author Robert Louis Stevenson wrote:

> I kept always two books in my pocket, one to read, one to write in. As I walked, my mind was busy fitting what I saw with appropriate words; when I sat by the roadside, I would either read or a pencil and a penny version-book would be in my hand, to note the features of the scene or commemorate some halting stanzas. Thus I lived with words.

We all want and need to be invited, to be included. So please accept our personal invitation to write your own affirmation story and to spend one week with us to boost your health, wealth, and happiness.

And here's our challenge to those receiving this invitation: Affirm your worth, exercise faith in your future, and accept this invitation. If, at any time during this process, you truly feel you are not moving forward, that you were better off before, that you are receiving no benefit or blessing from becoming worthy of success, health, wealth, and happiness—simply back off and back out and go back to your old ways and your old self.

But please know: In going back, you turn your back on those who have your back. Their love for you merits acceptance of this invitation. So, start now along this path of progression. We want only what is best for you.

WHY BE AN AUTHOR?

Being an author builds your authenticity, authority, and legacy. In a sense, you are like a mother—you suffer in order to bring new life and light into the world. Your writing, especially your finished and published or produced works, are like your children, part of your family, your posterity and legacy. You conceive them, carry them full term, and deliver them, resisting the temptation to abort or abbreviate natural gestation.

We make it easy for you to become a co-creator of this book by writing your own affirmation chapter or writing your own book or writing in our companion journal.

We first learned the value of this practice from education consultant Walter Gong and his three-person teaching concept: the teacher mentors the learner, and then the learner becomes a teacher of the content to others who repeat the cycle. One of our mentors, Stephen R. Covey, suggested the learner first capture the essence of the content, teach it to others, and then creatively expand on it. And that's what we invite you to do.

WHY BECOME A FINISHER?

A finisher is one who often competes and completes what he or she starts, bringing good works to fruition or conclusion. Of what might you and I be the finisher?

- We might be the finisher of agriculture (garden, farm, grove) and grow fruit/produce.
- We might be the finisher of culture (family, organization, company, church).
- We might be the finisher of good works (homes, projects, construction).
- We might be the finisher of sales, goals, dreams, and aspirations.
- We might be the finisher of this book, or your own book.

Now that you've started this book, we encourage you to commit to finishing it.

Why be a finisher? Unless you finish and deliver results, your returns on your investments of time, effort, and money are minimal.

Also, several people watch us and observe our faith, conduct, and work. We are surrounded by them, as spectators in a stadium. They are witnesses of us and to us of faith and endurance. Hence, they have the spirit of martyrs—the root of the ancient Greek word translated as witnesses. So, think of a finisher you admire and affirm: *I Am* a finisher!

CHRIST AS AUTHOR AND FINISHER

We might look to Jesus Christ as the best example of an author and finisher...particularly of our faith. The Greek word translated as "author" in Hebrews 12:2 can also mean originator, creator, captain, champion, chief, leader, or prince. Christ is our advocate and champion who perfects our faith, and because of the joy that awaited him on the far side of atonement, he endured the excruciating pain of the garden and the cross.

In his epistle to the Hebrews, Paul implores us to "lay aside every weight and sin and run with endurance the race set before us." He envisions a large group or "great cloud" of witnesses cheering us on. These heavenly or angelic spectators may be previous champions of faith who are cheering us as we seek to overcome opposition, obstacles, and discouragement.

Paul imagined himself as a runner who had a race to finish, and nothing could keep him from finishing the race. Just as Paul had his race to run, each of us has our own—and God calls us to finish it with joy and with endurance.

We affirm: Christ is the author and finisher of our faith: He was with us at the start; he is with us all along the way; and he will be with us at the finish line, for "he employs no servant" at the gates of heaven. With divine help and guidance, we can all finish what we start, if not in this life, then in the eternities to come as we learn to master the art of living.

> *"The master in the art of living makes little distinction between his work and his play, his labor and his leisure, his mind and his body, his information and his recreation, his love and his religion. He hardly knows which is which. He simply pursues his vision of excellence at whatever he does, leaving others to decide whether he is working or playing. To him he's always doing both."*
>
> — James A. Michener

WHY AFFIRM BY SAYING *I AM*?

What are the two most powerful words in any language?

The two most powerful words are *I Am* because what comes after *I Am* shapes your life. What you think or speak after *I Am* and especially what you believe after *I Am* will influence your choices and decisions. If you believe "*I Am* powerful," you are powerful!

Why is this so? When we affirm using the phrase *I Am*, we affirm our inherent familial connection to the divine, to a Heavenly Father and Mother, to a supernal presence and power.

The phrase "*I Am* that *I Am*" is derived from the Hebrew Bible, specifically the book of Exodus 3:14, where God uses it to refer to himself when speaking to Moses. God identifies himself as the "*I Am* that *I Am*"—communicating to Moses that he exists eternally, with neither a beginning nor an end similar to the sense of being.

The statement signifies the deity's self-existence and incommunicable sacredness. It exemplifies that God's being or essence surpasses human understanding, thus elevating his distinctiveness and transcendence. Essentially, it is God defining himself in a way that suggests spiritual sovereignty over everything, instilling hope and trust in his followers.

In the minds of the Jewish community, the *I Am* verse points to meeting God and being within his presence to encounter perfection and hence retrieve divine impartiality from the mercy of unconditional and universal love and influence. It demonstrates the irrefutably unchanging nature of the deity whom Judaism communes with. While no word in human language can fully encapsulate the essence of God, this *I Am* expression conveys much about Elohim.

In Christian practices, *I Am* also refers to the divinity of Jesus Christ, aka the Son of God. It signifies his divine nature in union with God, inseparable from the deity's holiness.

"*I Am* that *I Am*" is a strong declaration of Jehovah's existence and his unique connection with humanity. Jehovah simultaneously expresses that he himself decides upon his identity, indicating that his sense of his timeless presence is beyond our comprehension. Through this *I Am* declaration, every person is invited to affirm: I have faith in Christ.

This centrality of God on our path can inspire humility and remind us of our purpose: to align our heart and mind to divine truths by rebuking any counterintuitive agenda aiming to bind ourselves to trails of worldly possessions while reaffirming our identity and significance as uniquely facilitated by our maker. Conclusively, this phrase serves as a source for devout inspiration and eternal purpose, promoting the endless expansion of our spiritual journey.

For example, think of the affirmation in Revelation 22:13 uttered by Jesus Christ, "*I Am* alpha and omega" (the first and last letters of the Greek alphabet), the first and the last, the beginning and the end. Indeed, he was in the beginning, and he will be there in the end. What he starts, he finishes—ensuring that all creation serves and fulfills its intended purpose.

In the gospel of John alone, Christ makes seven *I Am* statements:

1. I am the bread of life. (6:35)
2. I am the light of the world. (8:12)
3. I am the door. (10:7)
4. I am the good shepherd. (10:11, 14)
5. I am the resurrection and the life. (11:25)
6. I am the way, the truth, and the life. (14:6)
7. I am the true vine. (15:1)

All of these metaphors reflect how he cares for us. Recall the story of the exodus, when the Israelites fled Egypt and the Lord held back the water so the people could cross the sea safely on dry ground, saving them from death. And then he provided daily manna (bread) to them in their wilderness. Likewise, he continues to provide the *bread of life* for the soul-hungry today. Jesus was born in Bethlehem, which means "house of bread." He said, "*I Am* the living bread (and living water). He who eats of this bread (and drinks of this water) will live forever."

When asked who he was, Jesus replied, "*I Am who I Am*. Before Abraham was born, *I Am*." The Jews clearly understood that he was declaring himself to be the Son of God incarnate. If not true, his statement would be blasphemy, punishable by death. But Jesus committed no blasphemy; he is the Son of God, the Messiah, our savior and redeemer.

And yet, in spite of our creation as beings of light, we occasionally experience and experiment with negative attitudes and self-defeating actions and affirmations.

MEANING OF *I AM*

The phrase I Am carries great significance in various ancient languages. For example, here are four translations of I Am:

- Hebrew: I Am is translated as "אוה ינא" (pronounced *Ani Hu*) and conveys not only that *I exist* but also that *I exist with God*—to be present, to be active, to create, to express myself, and to identify myself with God, the Great *I Am*.
- Greek: I Am is translated as "εἰμαι" (pronounced *eimai*). It conveys the state of being, existence, and self-expression.
- Sanskrit: I Am can be translated as "अहं अस्मि" (pronounced *Aham Asmi*). It represents the affirmation of a person's existence and self-awareness.
- Indo-European: While the translation varies slightly across these languages, the phrase generally conveys self-identity and existence.

Each ancient language is rich and nuanced, and the true essence of *I Am* goes beyond a simple translation. *I Am* represents the fundamental expression of self-awareness, existence, and personal affirmation, which transcends linguistic boundaries.

Let's say we asked you, "Who are you?" How might you respond using a positive *I Am* affirmation? You and I are entitled to use and reuse the power of the affirmative *I Am* to access our creative powers and finish what we start.

SEVEN *I AM* AFFIRMATIONS

Dan: While we name only seven affirmations, each of them could have many different variations. In fact, I have made many affirmations over the years. For example, I have often affirmed: *I Am* nature's greatest miracle. *I Am* having the greatest day of my life. *I Am* living and loving with passion. *I Am* attracting abundant blessings. *I Am* receiving inspired ideas and dreams in my heart and mind.

In the second section of this book, we make three affirmations to win the morning by exercising creativity and positivity. In the third section, we make three more affirmations to win the day and week. And the seventh affirmation empowers us to finish well and win the week and life.

WIN THE MORNING | Creativity and Positivity

AFFIRMATION 1: I Am an Author and Creator.

Writer, Speaker, Starter, Artist, Creative, Resourceful, Visionary, Divine, Light

AFFIRMATION 2: I Am Intentional and Innovative.

Proactive, Patient, Industrious, Opportunistic, Committed,

Purposeful, Vision- and Mission-Driven, Begin with the end in mind

AFFIRMATION 3: I Am Present and Positive.

Focused, Prescient, Enlightened, Alert, Aware, Alive, Empathic, Considerate, Loving, Optimistic, Filled with Hope and Faith

WIN THE DAY | Character and Competence

AFFIRMATION 4: I Am Worthy and Deserving.

Favored, Chosen, Blessed, Abundant, Unique, Grateful, Prayerful, Clean, Wise, Servant, Friend, Provider, Protector, Missionary, Child of God

AFFIRMATION 5: I Am Qualified and Capable.

Prepared, Strong, Powerful, Intelligent, Coach, Teacher, Reader, Leader, Motivator, Builder, Winner, Bold, Fearless, Courageous, Gifted, Skilled

AFFIRMATION 6: I Am Compassionate and Empathetic.

Loving, Accepting, Caring, Considerate, Charitable, Benevolent, Generous, Kind

WIN THE WEEK AND YOUR LIFE | Fitness and Sustainability

AFFIRMATION 7: I Am Fit and a Finisher Who Endures to the End.

Energetic, Healthy, Athletic, Happy, Joyful, Diligent, Disciplined, Unstoppable, Force of Nature, Determined, Persistent, Resilient

AFFIRMATION IN ACTION

Could you add a word to finish the following sentence?: I will be a finisher of this book because it could have ________________ impact on my life.

SUMMARY

- It is important to finish what you start.
- You can be an author or co-creator of this book and anything else you focus your energy on.
- God and Christ define themselves in the Bible as *I Am*, meaning they exist.
- You as a child of God can also use *I Am* to define yourself because you exist with God.
- You can use the seven affirmations in this book to win the morning, the day, the week, and life.

We invite you to finish what you start. *I Am* a starter, creator, and finisher. We invite you to be a co-creator of this book by sharing your unique ideas, stories, and thoughts in your journal as an addition to this book.

— CHAPTER 3 —

META-AFFIRMATION: *I AM* HEALING

"Some people cannot be cured, but everyone can heal."

— Author Unknown

The meta-affirmation and metaphor in this book is this: *I Am* healing. In effect, all seven affirmations deal with healing.

> Whatever my current illnesses, injuries, challenges, and past mistakes and sins, *I Am* now healing. My wounds are closing and my pain abating. *I Am* healing from all addictions, obsessions, losses, pains, and injuries.
>
> *I Am* healing, and with each passing day, *I Am* becoming stronger and more resilient. *I Am* learning to let go of the pain of the past, and *I Am* embracing the present moment with love and gratitude.
>
> *I Am* embracing my body as a sacred vessel, and *I Am* taking care of it with tenderness and respect. *I Am* releasing any negative thoughts or beliefs that do not serve me, and *I Am* replacing them with thoughts of love and positivity.
>
> *I Am* feeling empowered and supported, and *I Am* surrounded by loving friends and family members who offer me uncon-

ditional love and support. *I Am* grateful for every moment of my life, and *I Am* filled with joy and happiness.

I Am experiencing a new sense of inner peace and balance and aligning myself with healing energy every day. *I Am* tapping into my intuition and listening to my inner voice, which leads me on the path to healing and wholeness.

I Am letting go of any self-doubt or limiting beliefs that have held me back in the past, and *I Am* stepping into my power with confidence and courage. *I Am* discovering new strength within myself, and *I Am* amazed by the limitless possibilities before me.

I Am seeing the blessings that emerge from difficult experiences, and *I Am* learning valuable lessons that empower me to create a better future. I have the power to choose my path, and I choose to walk the path of healing and growth. *I Am* reminded every day of my strength and resilience, and *I Am* proud of myself for overcoming difficult challenges. I accept myself for who *I Am*, and I love myself completely.

I Am healing, and *I Am* becoming the best version of myself. *I Am* grateful for this journey of growth and transformation, and *I Am* excited to see what the future holds. With each passing moment, *I Am* becoming stronger, more confident, and more joyful.

As I feel sorrow and seek to make restitution for my mistakes and sins, *I Am* forgiving myself, being forgiven by others, and becoming clean and whole.

We affirm that love, forgiveness, repentance, and respect heal.

"We do not heal the past by dwelling there. We heal the past by living in the present."

— Marianne Williamson

THE HEALING PROMISE

We believe we can be healed, and prosper, for such is the promise in two passages in Jeremiah and one in Exodus.

> Jeremiah 30:17: "I will restore health unto thee, and I will heal thee of thy wounds," saith the LORD.
>
> Jeremiah 29:11: "For I know the plans I have for you," declares the Lord, "plans to prosper you and not to harm you, plans to give you hope and a future."
>
> Exodus 15:26: "I Am the LORD that heals thee."

Dan: Two affirmations, in particular, caused us to ponder the healing promise. One is the story of a friend named Roz. She started her direct sales journey the same week she was diagnosed with a brain tumor. The second is my daughter Crystal. She was diagnosed with a rare disease called Susac Syndrome that attacks the ears, eyes, and brain. Both women have since healed.

For this book, we have identified Seven Spotlights, one for each of the Seven Affirmations. These Seven Spotlights feature the fulfillment of the healing promise—real struggles with real-life challenges being overcome with affirmations, visualizations, and faith.

SPOTLIGHT: ROZ HOBBS
AFFIRMATION: I AM HEALING

Roz Hobbs had been healthy all her life and had been engaged in personal development since her early twenties when a friend introduced her to the book *Psycho-Cybernetics* by Maxwell Maltz. "When I read it, I was hooked," she recalls. "And the more involved I became with self-discovery, the more I thought differently. My life was good, and I was grateful for everything in my life."

But in 2007, Roz's condition changed. "I started experiencing some 'little things.' I'd look at the fireplace or chair, and I couldn't find a word for these things. I'd say, "I don't know what this is, but I'm not giving it any energy. I just want to move forward."

Then, on December 30, 2007, she went to her mom's birthday party and ducked under a marble table to pick something up. She hit the side of her head and fell backward. "I touched my head, and thought, *No blood. I'm okay. Let's go!* but I had a weird feeling in my head."

On January 1, 2008, the feeling intensified. "I went to see a doctor. He thought it was a minor concussion and just told me to watch it. But soon it was all over my head. I wondered what was going on, but I didn't want to give fear any energy or think any negative thought."

The next morning, Roz went to see her doctor and had a scan. "After my scan, I was casually waiting when my name was called, and a band put on my arm. The emergency room doctor told me I had a tumor, a glioblastoma. Since I work in the heath field, I was familiar with that tumor, and I knew it was usually a death sentence.

"I blocked out what the doctor said next. It was like; I don't want to hear scary or feel fear. I want to focus on what I need to focus on. I decided that it didn't matter what the diagnosis was, I was going to beat it and be healthy. I was going to keep my thoughts positive and focus on what I needed to do. I started listening to *The Secret* every morning, and I grabbed onto certain affirmations: *I Am* grateful. *I Am* cancer free. *I Am* healthy."

At first, Roz didn't realize the power in affirmations, but when she started doing them, she saw how affirmations stick, as long as the belief is there.

Three weeks went by before Roz met with Dr. Fox, a neurosurgeon. He told her, "Yes, you have a tumor. It's a meningioma, and it's benign."

"I looked at my husband Lindsey and thought to myself, *This is easy*. I had no fear. I thought, *The good Lord is not ready to take me*. I believed I would be given a second chance and that I had more work to do in my life."

On the day of the surgery, Roz learned that her surgeon Dr. Fox had referred her to Dr. Steinke, the best neurosurgeon ever, a specialist in brain cancer surgery. "When I met him, he interviewed me, and I interviewed him. I wanted to have a connection. I needed for him to be on my side and for us to be on the same page."

Dr. Steinke wheeled her into the operating room where there were about fifteen people—doctors and nurses—and every camera had a picture of her tumor. "I said out loud, 'This is all for me?!' I felt I was in great hands and loaded with prayer and positivity."

When Roz woke up after the surgery, she could sense people hustling around her, and she started to cry. "They asked if I was in pain, and I said, 'No, I'm just so happy.' It was like I'd done all of this mental and emotional work, and here I was waking up. Then, I fell back asleep."

Dr. Steinke called Lindsey to let him know the surgery went well. Then he said, "I have to tell you, Lindsey, that I've never experienced this before. The first words out of your wife's mouth were '*I Am* awesome.'"

Dr. Fox came to see Roz and said, "Look at you! You're even talking."

Before the surgery, Roz was told, "You might need to learn to talk and walk again."

That night, Roz had inflammation on the brain and was given drugs. She got through the night and woke up feeling like a million bucks. "I was taking my supplements and walking around the ICU. They were watching me carefully, surprised that I was doing so well. They kept me in ICU a few days, and then moved me to another room in the hospital. I said, 'I'm ready to go home!' When they sent me home, they ordered, "no mental stimulation and as much darkness as possible.'"

For the next two months, Roz slept a lot. "Lindsey cooked all my meals. He'd wake me up to have something to eat, and then I'd sleep again. It was fine; the brain was healing. Then I got permission to go for walks outside. Thank goodness [my income stream was uninterrupted]; I didn't have to worry about finances or anything—just focus on *I Am* healing.

Surgery was done to relieve pressure on the brain. The tumor was wrapped around the main artery and there was nothing doctors could do but keep doing surgeries.

Three months later, Roz went to see Dr. Steinke. He showed her a picture of her brain. "Before, my brain was darker in color with some black spots," said Roz. "This picture showed my brain lighter in color, not a blemish—pristine."

June 23, 2011 was Roz's last surgery, and a year later, the tumor had not grown back. "I was healthy! I challenged myself to climb Mt. Kilimanjaro! Last year [in 2022], I hiked through Patagonia, and this year [2023], I'm doing Mt. Everest base camp. I'm doing three mountains at the same time."

Roz now affirms: "*I Am* grateful for my blessings. *I Am* lucky because I feel I've been given so many great things in my life. My affirmations paid big dividends for me when my life truly depended upon it. *I Am* fortunate. I feel God was giving me a second chance. Perhaps I needed to be more grateful. I thank the Lord every morning for giving me another day. We all talk about life being precious, but we don't live thinking life is precious."

Daily, Roz affirms: "*I Am* awesome. *I Am* cancer free. *I Am* happy. *I Am* blessed. And when my health returned, I affirmed, *I Am* ready to go to work."

"I hope my story can bring strength to people, and have them believe that anything is possible," says Roz. "In my case, so many little things happened that were gifts of God. People were brought into my life. God does know best, and he is going to bless us—over time. I feel fortunate and feel I have a purpose—to invite others to have faith in the power of positive energy and affirmations."

Dan: I started my fascination with affirmations many years ago when I read Og Mandino's book *The Greatest Salesman in the World* and studied his Ten Scrolls. In particular, I was drawn to the Scroll IV affirmation: *I Am* nature's greatest miracle. It reads in part:

> Since the beginning of time, never has there been another person with my mind, my heart, my eyes, my hands, my hair, my mouth. None that came before, none that live today, and none that comes tomorrow can walk and talk and move and think exactly like me. All men are my brothers, yet *I Am* different from each. *I Am* a unique creature.
>
> Within me burns a flame which has been passed from generations uncounted and its heat is a constant irritation to my spirit to become better than *I Am*, and I will. I will fan this flame of dissatisfaction and proclaim my uniqueness to the world.

I read that scroll over and over again, assimilated its truth, and made that affirmation thousands of times. As a result, I see myself and others as nature's greatest miracle.

I later learned that Og Mandino had studied the life of Benjamin Franklin. Franklin kept a journal and asked himself each morning, "What good shall I do this day?" Then he reflected each evening, "What good have I done today?" Franklin created a list of thirteen virtues to develop his character, and weekly he focused on one virtue with the aim to make it a habit.

Sadly, few young people today make positive affirmations daily. For instance, each year I visit Mission Viejo High School in California. There a terrific teacher named Brent Pillsbury imbues his students with character, education, and inspiration. He connects with business leaders in the community and invites them to share their insights on life and business.

In April 2023, I visited Brent's classroom for the seventh year in a row. Some students made eye contact; others were more cautious to engage. After going through my introduction to self-help, amazing mentors, and influential books, I paused and asked if any of them used affirmations.

Only one student—an amazing fifteen-year-old named Chloe—raised her hand. Chloe said that she uses affirmations every day. "I wake up every morning and tell myself "*I Am* capable."

This was an awesome share for the class and for me since at the time, I was writing this book, which seeks to have countless people at every age co-create with us on the *I Am* journey.

Ken: The essence of the Seven Affirmations is this: we progress exponentially faster by focusing on one specific affirmation each day and by making seven positive and powerful affirmations each week, week after week.

I came to realize more fully the power of *I Am* Affirmations when I was invited by the CEO of IAMS (pet foot company) to visit their new corporate office in Ohio. When I arrived, I was impressed with the new facility and its expansive and impressive entry. Shortly after entering, I was greeted in the most friendly and welcoming manner by the company receptionist. She was a gorgeous blonde, with bright eyes and a broad smile, and impeccably groomed. She shook my hand and then gave me a kiss on cheek. Next, she introduced me to her assistant, and I told her I had an appointment with the CEO. The receptionist then led me to his office.

As you may have guessed, this exceptional receptionist at IAMS was a dog, a Golden Retriever, trained to meet, greet, and welcome visitors. And she wore a necklace with an affirmation that read: *I Am* the IAMS Receptionist.

I have often reflected on the affirming power of *I Am* affirmations and on the empowering trust that IAMS invested in their loyal and friendly canine receptionist.

AFFIRMATION: I CAN DO IT

Most of us are born positive with a predisposition to be proactive—to take initiative and reasonable risks, affirming "I can do it!" It's how we all learn to walk, talk, and do things from birth to age five or when institutions start imposing their norms on us.

Ken: I, too, was born positive; at least that's the testimony of my mother and the evidence gleaned from baby and child photos. It seems I was always smiling for the camera. Positivity was both natural and was nurtured in my nature-nurture culture.

One of the favorite books my wife Pam and I read to our three sons is the classic *The Little Engine That Could* by Watty Piper. We must have read it to each of them 100 times or more, always acting out scenes, complete with the train noises.

I think that book did more good for our boys than school and church combined because it encapsulated the principles of Applied Positive Psychology (APP). It gave them the can-do attitude—the positive affirmation of capability and visualization of desired results:

I Think I Can
I Think I Should
I Have a Plan
I Knew I Could

I recall the line by Ralph Waldo Emerson: "That which we persist in doing becomes easier to do, not that the nature of the thing has changed but our power to do has increased."

And I'm reminded of this wisdom:

> Stick to your task until it sticks to you,
> Beginners are many, finishers are few.

This has been my mantra over the years. I'm not that bright, but I put in the work, even at night by candlelight. When I feel like the goal or the task I face is unreachable, *I Am* still willing to start in faith and see how far I can go. Now, after fifty-five years of professional experience, I have the benefit of hindsight. I see clearly how sticking to my tasks—my jobs, my books, my magazines, my marriage and family relationships—with faith, patience, perseverance, sacrifice, hard work, and affirmation—has paid off in rich rewards (not all financial).

Dan: In writing this book, we have come to know many amazing people who practice daily affirmations. For instance, Nigel Henry affirms: *I Am* a peacemaker. He notes:

> Personal Peace is a personal choice. Three letters, I - A - M, form two powerful words, I and Am, and those words can be used in two different orders. Used in one way, *I Am*, the words create commitment and conviction. When the letters are reversed, *Am I?*, they ask a question and can create doubt and discouragement.
>
> For example, *Am I* good enough? *Am I* doing enough? *Am I* worthy?
>
> Self-assessment is a good thing. Unfortunately, the *Am I* question often turns self-assessment into self-doubt and negative self-talk.

> Paraphrasing Proverbs 23, As I think in my heart, so am I.
> Or said in a non-Star Wars Yoda way, *I Am*, as I think in my heart.
> So, I encourage you to affirm: *I Am*...peaceful, a peacemaker, at peace.
> The *I Am* statement is a declaration of your identity and an affirmation of your intention. The affirmation is the start to having personal peace and being a peacemaker.

And Troy Thompson uses affirmations to clarify his Identity and Purpose. He writes:

> *I Am* a child of God. *I Am* a beloved son of God. I find peace in Christ.

He notes, however, that "having peace doesn't mean my life will always be peaceful, without drama or trial. It means having peace despite circumstances. Even when I have peace in Christ, the storms will still come. But when I build upon the rock, having a firm foundation in Christ, I can have peace despite my circumstance. Many things will happen that are out of my control. Still, I can have peace when I focus on and put energy into what I can control today."

MASTERS OF AFFIRMATIONS: LOU TICE AND PETE CARROLL

Ken: I came to know Lou Tice, the master of daily affirmations (smart self-talk), in 1993 when I was invited to fly to Seattle and meet with Lou and his wife Diane at their estate home that backed down to Lake Washington. We sat in his elegant study, talked of how we might help each other, and quickly agreed to work together. So, for two days each month over the next two years, I consulted with them in Seattle and flew to other parts of the world to meet with their associates.

I was also invited to their ranch on the other side of the Cascades where I became friends with football coach Pete Carroll (NY Jets, USC, Seattle Seahawks), who uses the power of positive affirmations to lead his teams to national championships and Super Bowls.

So, how did Lou Tice, this dirt poor Irish-Catholic kid and former high school football coach, become a wealthy speaker and trainer of leadership teams worldwide? He imagined it, envisioned it, and affirmed it daily!

In 1970, Lou was a high-school teacher and football coach, struggling to pay the bills and raise a rapidly growing family on $1,000 month. (Diane and Lou had adopted or become foster parents to seven children, many of whom had been physically or psychologically abused.)

Lou said, "We treated them as we believed they deserved to be treated, as uniquely valuable, lovable human beings, but we faced major behavioral problems because they had gone through experiences that had convinced them of three things: they were deeply flawed and unworthy; the world was a painful place; and adults were the source of pain and could not be trusted. People act in accordance with the truth, as they believe and perceive it to be. We move toward and become like that which we think about—our present thoughts determine our future. Our kids' treatment and surroundings had changed, but their picture of who they were had not changed."

One day, on a family road trip to Portland, Diane had the children imagine their ideal home in specifics. As the kids imagined things, she wrote them down. Twenty years later, she found her notes. Between their home and ranch, they had every item on the list, along with a strong marriage and a respected international company. Diane Tice used the same power of imagination and positive affirmation and self-talk to beat what was called "terminal" cancer.

I learned to become a possibility thinker, someone who looks beyond conventions and conditions, by focusing not on what I don't want—the problems, obstacles, and difficulties—but by focusing on the options, solutions, and innovations that give me the results I do want.

I learned I was living with dangerous blind spots or scotomas that were causing me to see what I expected to see, hear what I expected to hear, and experience what I expected to experience. Scotomas block positive change efforts, flexibility, and creativity because they keep us prisoners to preconceived ways of seeing things and habitual ways of doing things. When we lock on to our truth, we lock out other possibilities unless we engage in smart self-talk.

SEVEN AFFIRMATION CORRELATIONS: SEVEN VISUALIZATIONS, SEVEN HABITS, SEVEN DAYS

Our Seven Affirmations correlate with Seven Visualizations, with *The 7 Habits of Highly Effective People* by Stephen R. Covey, and with the seven days of the week.

CORRELATION WITH SEVEN VISUALIZATIONS

Visualizations, along with affirmations, have a long and rich history, rooted in ancient spiritual practices and modern psychological research and sports psychology.

Visualization is a vital companion to affirmation: In effect, you are seeing and feeling what you are saying, which has twice the impact. Seeing yourself being and doing what you are saying and affirming attracts that new reality or new normal closer to you, one day at a time, consistent with and in harmony with Mother Nature and Father Time or natural laws and governing principles.

While there may be disruptions and setbacks to what you are seeing, saying, and feeling, over time you will experience more of what you express in imagination and intention.

By practicing these simple yet powerful affirmations and visualizations every day, we can overcome negative self-talk and limiting beliefs, reprogram our mindset and paradigm, and cultivate a greater sense of well-being, success, and inner peace.

For example, here are Seven Visualizations that support the Seven Affirmations:

I AM **Affirmation**	**Visualization**
1: Author/Creator	I see myself authoring, inventing, innovating, and creating things in line with my talents, gifts, abilities, duties, roles, and goals.
2: Intentional/Innovative	I see myself making plans and goals for initiating projects and being resourceful and intentional in making innovations.
3: Present/Positive	I see myself being fully present and positive when relating with people and in performing tasks, playing sports, or working.
4: Worthy/Deserving	I see myself becoming more worthy and deserving of the blessings and benefits I seek.
5: Qualified/Capable	I see myself becoming and being highly qualified, capable, and competent in my personal and professional pursuits.
6: Compassionate/ Empathetic	I see myself becoming more worthy and deserving of the blessings and benefits I seek.
7: Fit/Finisher	I envision myself maintaining fitness and crossing the finish line to the cheers of family members, friends, and fans.
1-7: *I Am* Healing	I see my wounds closing, my body healing, my soul being whole.

CORRELATION WITH COVEY'S SEVEN HABITS

Our Seven Affirmations also correlate closely with Covey's Seven Habits. Habits 1-3 focus on personal effectiveness (private victory), moving from dependence to independence. Habits 4-6 emphasize effectiveness through collaboration and communication (public victory), moving from independence to interdependence. And Habit 7 is focused on continuous growth, renewal, and sustainability. Likewise, our Seven Affirmations provide inside-out application to personal and professional growth and development, day by day and week by week. Affirmations 1-3 focus on winning the morning; Affirmations 4-6 deal with winning the day; and Affirmation 7 encourages creative renewal to heal, be whole, and win the week, week after week, thereby winning your life!

CORRELATION WITH SEVEN DAYS OF THE WEEK

Our Seven Affirmations also correlate with the seven days of the week, which constitute one development cycle—a cycle that repeats itself with different and various applications. As you affirm good feeling and good fortune, you can escape many traps, debunk myths, cast off the burdens that weigh you down, and become free to fly—not like the mythical Icarus who flew too close to the sun and melted away, but fly by the sight and light of the sun, moon, and stars—from one Sunday to the next—and progress each day and each week.

Here's our bold promise: Devote one week with us, Affirmation Week, and you will experience Whole Health and Whole Wealth and establish the pattern for your new life. It just requires an eighteen-minute commitment each morning for a week with us to super-charge your results.

Proverbs 28: 1: The wicked flee…but the righteous are bold as a lion.

AFFIRMATION IN ACTION

Make the following **I Am** affirmation: **I Am** absolutely committed to completing this Affirmation Week.

SUMMARY

- Love, forgiveness, repentance, and respect heal.
- God does know best, and he is going to bless us—over time.
- Tell yourself "I can do it." Perseverance will pay off with rich rewards.
- You can have peace when you focus on and put energy into what you can control today.
- Become a possibility thinker—rather than focus on what you don't want, focus on the options, solutions, and innovations that give you the results you want.

— CHAPTER 4 —

WELCOME TO AFFIRMATION WEEK

"You do not rise to the level of your goals, you fall to the level of your systems."
— James Clear

In this book, we condense your life into the compact timeframe of one week, one whole week, for two good reasons: first, to show you that your week is the pattern of your life; second, to show you that how well you live one week can make a big difference in your life.

We invite you to divide your week differently: Instead of having your week begin on Monday and end on Friday (Work Week) and then having a two-day Weekend on Saturday and Sunday, start Affirmation Week on a Sunday (Creation Sunday) and then enjoy five days of field "play" (you never really "work" again). And your week ends on Saturday for recreation.

Work Week is the counterfeit of Wealth Week. In any Work Week, you work and work and then you end. In that sense, it's like a slow death, week by week.

In contrast, with Wealth Week, you never "work" and you never "end." You create and play, recreate and renew, multiply and replenish. You start a new pattern of health and wealth that continues week after week. How your week starts greatly influences how your week ends—and whether or not your wealth and health pattern ever even begins.

How wealthy will you become in one week? We don't know exactly, but you can make an intelligent guess—by extending the patterns of your life (patterns embedded in your current week). Your past and present are prologue to your future. They predict your future, but they do not predetermine your future. You determine your future—your agency, choices, and actions.

As Ebenezer Scrooge said in Charles Dickens' *A Christmas Carol*: "Men's courses foreshadow certain ends, to which, if persevered in, they must lead. But if the courses be departed from, the ends will change."

Yes, things tend to remain the same (stasis)—meaning this week will be like the last week and next week—unless you do a few things differently. Whole Health and Wealth are the natural outcomes of how you live your days in the context of your week, month, and year.

One Week is one full circle or cycle, a pattern that repeats: having fifty-two cycles of learning a year, you will have fifty-two patterns and will accelerate progress and results, be more responsive to the conditions and opportunities before you, and use available resources more effectively.

Instead of having one lifetime, year, or month in which to become wealthy, you have one week (and week after week). Weekly, ask yourself: What have I/we learned last week that we can apply this week? What should be continued, stopped, or started?

TRY FOR ONE DAY, WEEK, MONTH

With daily positive affirmations, you can create a new habit in one month—and maintain it. Once you make it through the initial conditioning phase, it becomes easier to sustain. So, do it daily for thirty days to form the habit, perhaps with a friend or coach, using visualization (seeing yourself performing the new habit and enjoying positive results) and using daily affirmation.

Again, the aim of Affirmation Week is to provide a pattern and process for making consistent progress, week after week, to move beyond stasis and paralysis by planting and then harvesting seeds of faith that result in sustainable organic growth.

Our bold promise of the payoff is this: By making daily *I Am* affirmations, you start receiving higher returns on your investments, as you experience growth, progress, and positive change. The direction of your life (where you go and what you do) will align with who you are (your true identity). Your vision and values will inform your mission, roles, and goals. You'll be empowered to lead others. You'll live daily with peace of mind, joy, wisdom, purpose, and passion. You'll experience a sense of progress and exponential ROI.

Here's your bottom-line choice: Either waste another week of your life by starting your week on Monday and looking forward to a weekend of diversion (a vicious cycle) or invest one week to create a virtuous cycle—a wealth/health spiral that continues indefinitely.

AFFIRMATION IN ACTION

My identity is changing now! Can you be specific—*right now*—and complete the following statement about your identity?:

My identity is what I consistently give my focus to, which is ____________.

SUMMARY

- Start Affirmation Week on a Sunday (Creation Sunday).
- Think of it as Wealth Week, not Work Week.
- Weekly ask yourself, "What have I/we learned last week that we can apply this week? What should be continued, stopped, or started?"
- By making daily *I Am* affirmations, you start receiving higher returns on your investments, as you experience growth, progress, and positive change.

SECTION II

WIN THE MORNING
Creativity and Positivity

In this section, we make three affirmations to "win the morning" by exercising creativity and positivity. How well we start often determines how well we finish.

AFFIRMATION 1: *I Am* a Creator.

AFFIRMATION 2: *I Am* Intentional.

AFFIRMATION 3: *I Am* Present.

— CHAPTER 5 —

I AM A CREATOR

"Make an empty space in any corner of your mind, and creativity will instantly fill it."

— Dee Hock

DAY 1
I AM A CREATOR **Author, Writer, Speaker, Starter, Artist, Creative, Resourceful, Visionary, Divine, Light**

WELCOME TO SUNDAY

Why start Affirmation Week on Sunday? Monday starts the work week, and you are no longer working for a living or living to work—you are playing to win for yourself and for others. Money is just part of your mission—your means to a much bigger end in mind. Creation Sunday is the day when you determine what that greater mission should be. And you envision a plan or path to get there. No vision and no plan results in another week mostly wasted!

The calendar week starts on Sunday, not Monday. Sunday is not half of the weekend. It's not the end of the old week, but the start of the new week—and the key to attaining and sustaining whole health and wealth. This view of Sunday isn't new—we're just restoring that orientation. So, on this Sunday of Creation, you see yourself in a new light—from the perspective of faith in the future, not fear of failure in the present or past. When you are clear on your *why* (your motive), you are motivated by the vision to fulfill your mission.

WHAT DOES IT MEAN TO BE "A CREATOR"?

Affirmation Week starts on "Creation Sunday" with the affirmation: *I Am* an author and creator. For us (Dan and Ken), the first Sunday of the month is a Fast Sunday, a day when we forego two meals in order to be filled with all that is good. We affirm that faith in our creativity makes the fountain of health and wealth flow. If you're not experiencing the universal dream of abundance, you're likely experiencing the impossible dream of scarcity.

While saying *I Am* a creator, see yourself creating or authoring something that aligns with your gifts, talents, intelligences, or strengths. Feel the emotions of having your work published or having your creations come to life.

You might also affirm: *I Am* a procreator (pro-creator) of children and of other "children," including "brainchildren." I bring good things to life. *I Am* life-affirming, earth-loving, and life-giving. My ability to procreate, co-create, and pro-create (be proactive in acts of creation) are my most prized gifts and powers, and I treat them with respect and responsibility. I also have the power to rescript—recognizing ineffective scripts written by others for me and changing those scripts by proactively writing new ones.

THE CREATOR AFFIRMATION IN ACTION

CORRELATION WITH COVEY'S HABIT 1: BE PROACTIVE

In Habit 1, Stephen R. Covey advises us to "be proactive," to take initiative, to be an author, to create and write our own scripts, and to change what we can change. When we are *reactive,* we allow our environment, circumstances, or other people to dictate how we feel and act. Being *proactive* empowers us to choose our thoughts and actions. As we take control of our actions and our responses to people and to our circumstances, we will be happier, healthier, more motivated, less stressed, and better able to communicate and solve problems. We choose to write the scripts by which we live our life. With self-awareness, we can be proactive and take responsibility for our choices. Reactive people take a passive stance—they believe things happen to them and say things like: There's nothing I can do. That's just the way *I Am.* They think the problem is "out there"—and that thought becomes the problem. They feel victimized and out of control. In contrast, proactive people accept responsibility: response-ability is the ability to choose how we respond to stimuli and to situations. We focus on the Circle of Influence that lies within our Circle of Concern by working on those things we can do something about. Positive energy expands our Circle of Influence.

ATOMIC HABITS CAN BECOME AUTOMATIC HABITS

James Clear, author of the bestseller *Atomic Habits,* outlines a clear process for being creative and connecting ideas: 1) gather material, 2) intensely work over the material in your mind, 3) step away from the problem, 4) allow the idea to come back to you naturally, and 5) test your idea in the real world and adjust it based on feedback.

And he affirms his clear motive: to empower, not to prescribe. "I'm not interested in telling you which habits you should build or which choices you should make. You know what works for your life and circumstances better than I ever could. Instead, I want to equip you with ideas and strategies so you can make your own choices and do the things you want to do. I'll give you the hammer—you decide where to drive the nail."

We share the same clear motive and encourage all who have a hammer to "drive the nail" for creative and constructive purposes. After all, we all know from experience that people who are good with a hammer tend to see everything and everybody as a nail. And so, it can become an atomic and automatic habit to hammer somebody or something!

Affirm that starting today, nothing will be the same—not your finances, your lifestyle, your work, your relationships—all of it will change. The only question is: Will you be coauthor (with God and others) of those changes, or merely one who is impacted by them? You have the capacity to create your future. In spite of your conditions and conditioning, you have choices (and choices have consequences). You can choose your response, gain emancipation from debt and debilitation, seek enlightenment, and become a powerful force for good.

As Steve Jobs said, "Being the richest man in the cemetery doesn't matter to me. Going to bed at night saying we've done something wonderful, that's what matters to me."

And as Benjamin Hardy writes: "The point of no return is the moment of full commitment, wherein your identity and energy shift from avoiding what you fear to fully approaching what you most deeply want."

SPOTLIGHT: MITZI VAUGHAN

When Mitzi was introduced to her current company, she was going through her second divorce. "I'd been diagnosed with melanoma and a brain aneurysm. I was a single mom of five kids, and my husband decided to quit his job—and leave us. I had no child support, was taking care of the kids (three of them were in sports), was working two jobs, and was a full-time college student. My parents lived out of state, so I was in survival mode, going through the motions and thinking, *I don't have time to be sick; I have to work because I'm the only income.*"

Mitzi was losing her home and lacked enough money to make a security deposit to rent an apartment. She wondered, "Where am I going to live? What am I going to do? I was looking at all the expenses, plus day care. No matter how much I worked, I couldn't afford my bills. I was sleeping about four hours a night."

One day, Mitzi's boss told her about a direct sales opportunity that she thought Mitzi would be good at. Mitzi replied, "I'm not a salesperson!" But she was also desperate to get healthy and change her life. "We were always eating on-the-go," she said. "Nothing was healthy about our lifestyle."

Then one day, two different doctors called her. One told her she had a brain aneurysm, and one told her she had melanoma. "I wondered, *Now, what do I do with myself?*"

This was the first time Mitzi had ever been introduced to direct sales. "I was a customer service manager, and I was terrified of sales. All I had ever wanted to be was a wife and mother. I had no career plans. I came from a big Catholic family. It was my plan to have lots of kids."

Mitzi tried a weight-loss program, lost seventeen pounds in thirty days, and felt amazing. "That's where I thought my journey would end. I had no intention of selling this product, but my boss kept talking to me, and I gave every excuse why I couldn't do it. I had negative self-talk: Why would anyone listen to anything I have to say? I've had two husbands cheat on me. I've moved numerous times with my kids because I couldn't afford where we were living. I've lost jobs when a kid would get sick. I have no belief in myself. I am humiliated. Nobody's ever going to want me. I'm a failure as a daughter, mother, and wife—a disappointment to my family. I'm embarrassed to talk to anybody. It was a constant cycle of struggle."

Luckily, the women in Mitzi's office were so wowed by her weight loss that they did the program, and Mitzi received some thank-you checks from the company for referring them.

Mitzi was then asked to make a simple commitment: Focus on helping four people get started. "I was afraid to call people on the phone. I would shake so bad I was almost hyperventilating—but I did it anyway. I just kept on going. I kept talking to people. I would even talk to people in an elevator. I would say something like, 'Do you keep your options open when it comes to making extra money?' I was fumbling over my words—but I did it anyway. And within a few months, I was earning an extra $3,000 a month. That was life changing."

And then the personal growth part of her journey began. "I started watching *The Secret.* Even if I was cooking dinner, or doing homework with the kids, I'd have it playing in the background. When I'd go to sleep, I'd have it playing. I was listening to this stuff about the Universe and trying to figure out how that coincides with my faith. I learned quickly that I was creating the world I was seeing. I was creating that reality. I was creating all the stuff in my life, and I had to be accountable for it."

Mitzi had lived with a victim mentality for many years. "Now, I was taking ownership of what I was creating," she said. "I was creating a different future for my family! So many things happened that first year. My ex-husband came in and tried to kidnap my kids. At the time, it was almost like I was living this fairytale life. My mindset was changing, and I started thinking, *Wow, I see so much potential! I can do so much good if I learn these principles and apply them.*"

Dan McCormick's friend, Freddy Elias, got Mitzi started with affirmations. He said, "Mitzi, I want you to say, *I Am* deserving; *I Am* worthy—but she could not say it because she did not feel worthy. He said, "I want you to write affirmations and look at yourself in the mirror and speak to them." But when Mitzi would look at herself in the mirror and say, "*I Am* beautiful," and "*I Am* a great mom," she did not believe it. "I felt like a failure for a long while."

But the more Mitzi said these affirmations, the more she thought, "What do I have to do to believe that? I'm saying *I Am* beautiful, but I'm looking at myself and not feeling beautiful. So, what would it take for me to feel beautiful? Working out, exercising, making better choices with what I eat and drink. The more consistent I was with an affirmation, the more I felt it and believed it. I wanted to be a great mom, and I wanted to be proud of myself. I wanted my kids to be proud of me, and to enjoy their life. They deserved so much more."

Mitzi did not believe she was a great mom or leader because her life was chaos. So, in order to affirm that, she asked herself, "What does a great leader do? They show up every day. They're consistent. So, I started doing affirmations consistently—every day. The more I did them, the more when I looked in the mirror and said, *I Am* a great leader, *I Am* a great mom, the more I started to believe it and feel it, and it made me feel good! Suddenly, I was on this virtuous cycle: *I Am* a truth-seeker. I began asking, 'What is the truth as to what *I Am* capable of becoming?' I started delving into 'Who am I?' and 'Who am I going to be?'

"I had to discover what that was," said Mitzi. "I learned that God will take your mess and make it a message for somebody. Instead of being ashamed of all those things—being thirty-five and divorced twice, being cheated on, feeling like I'm just never good enough—now I was taking my story and empowering people with it. So, after two-and-a-half years, I left the jobs I was working and did direct sales full time."

Mitzi felt like she was living on cloud nine, even though she was living in a two-bedroom condo with five kids! "But we were happy every day," she said. "And I learned the power of gratitude. *I Am* thankful for everything. Even if I was struggling with my bills, I'd write on the bill, 'I'm thankful this bill is paid.' I'd cut my grass and say, 'I'm so thankful I get to cut my grass.'"

The blessings kept multiplying; and within five years, she was earning six figures!

That's when she read *The Greatest Salesman in the World.* "I struggled with the word leadership. I couldn't see myself as a leader. I would compare myself to others who were great leaders and think, *I'm not any of the things that they are.* I read Scroll II [in the book], 'I will greet this day with love in my heart.' I always felt that love is my superpower; *I Am* good at loving people! I've never had a problem with not holding grudges or forgiving people. I could affirm: *I Am* loving people. *I Am* loving life. That came easy to me, so I thought, *Love is how I impact people and how I lead people. I can lead with love because that's what I'm good at.*"

Still, it took her five years before Mitzi could say, "I own my leadership." "I was constantly going through affirmations and creating a new identity, Mitzi 2.0! What does she look like, and who do I have to become to be her? I had to step out of the old identity and how other people thought of me. Now *I Am* my new identity. *I Am* becoming something more. *I Am* capable of helping other people."

At the end of the day, said Mitzi, "when I go to heaven and meet my creator, he will show me the best version of myself. So, I'm accessing that person, accessing that knowledge, accessing that wisdom and trying to step into that place. We can save people so much time if they know that they already have that divinity within them. Now, all we need to do is access it!

"*I Am* creating, and you are creating every day, and God is part of you," said Mitzi. "I thought God was this being in the sky that I pray to, but no. *I Am* one with God. *I Am* part of him. He's part of me, and through him *I Am* creating, showing up and able to do things."

Now, when Mitzi works out, trying to push herself to the next level, she says, "I can do all things through Christ who strengthens me."

"I started saying such things without even knowing what they meant, but I could feel the power in the words. The more you do it, the more you feel it, and embody it, and embrace it—the more you become it!"

HOW TO BECOME "A CREATOR" HOW'S YOUR VISION?

Visualization is the indispensable close companion of affirmation: We need to see ourselves (in our mind's eye) being, doing, and feeling what we are affirming. So, start your Affirmation Week by creating a crystal-clear vision.

In calibrating your life vision, you look beyond the "I" chart with the top line that reads "WIIFM?" (What's In It For Me?). What is ego-friendly is seldom eco-friendly.

You may find that you need glasses—a customized, personalized prescription for eyewear to correct your vision. You want your vision to be in focus. You want to see *20/20* and beyond the 2020s. However, as we age, cataracts may cloud the lenses in the eyes, which affects vision. The lens must be clear for the retina to receive a sharp image. If the lens is cloudy from a cataract, the image you see will be blurred. And hence, you can't see your way forward; you only have a glimpse or vague sense of your presence, purpose, and potential. So, you may settle for what little you can see, for far less than you could achieve with the same effort because you can't see the abundance awaiting you behind the curtain of adversity.

Life is about progression—making progress from one degree of life and light to another. And your creative vision drives your progression. Amazing people like J. K. Rowling, Walt Disney, and other creative geniuses envisioned entire worlds. We are all beneficiaries of visionaries who see a world that is simply different than the world in which others live—a world based on hope and optimism, a happy place, founded on the premise of being a force for good.

Elevation facilitates vision. So, if your vision is limited at ground level, climb to a mountaintop or temple—ascend and elevate. Beyond enjoying the view, capture the vision in a clean setting, in nature's temple, closer to the heavens and earthly creations.

We sense the abundance of life when we engage in creation. We all want to look back on life and feel that we have created something of value—and left others better because of our influence and made the world into a better place.

CARRY BAGGAGE OR SCRIPT A NEW PATTERN?

Can we really create something fresh and new when we carry so much baggage from the past? True, we all bring considerable baggage with us. So, is there any hope that we can change, heal, and grow? Become healthy, wealthy, and whole?

Yes, Mitzi proves it! But here's the deal: Beyond this week lies either another one just like the last or a new week patterned after your affirmations. The trick to living a Whole Life is to bring the best of your past—your true and authentic self—forward with you into your future and leave the rest (the dead weight) behind.

This is much easier said than done. In order to create a new and better future, you need a powerful new script. So, on Creation Sunday, become a script writer, and rewrite the story of your life; in fact, ***be the hero of your story***, as suggested by the lyrics in the musical *Big Fish*.

What is the story of your life, so far? Your life is a story that started even before you were born. As the author, you can write and rewrite the script and create your future. How do want your story to end? Start being the main character in your own life story by stepping into your starring role as leading actor and stop playing the role of extra or best supporting actor to someone else. Awakening to who you truly are, becoming your authentic self, is the best story you could ever write. So, express your dreams, values, passions, and creative ideas. Stop acting and conforming to another person's tastes, keeping silent when you have something to say, compromising your spirit, or staying in a bad situation out of fear. Move forward with faith toward the life of your dreams.

THE LIFE-CHANGING BENEFITS OF AFFIRMING "I AM A CREATOR" LIFE BEYOND LIMITATION

The Persian poet Hafiz wrote, "The words you speak become the house you live in," suggesting that our words shape our perceptions and beliefs, animate our behavior, and create our self-image; moreover, our words often become manifest in our works.

For many people, life is about loss, lack, limits, and liabilities. So, they find it hard to imagine a life beyond limitation. With myopic vision, we see only what is imminent or proximate—what is about to happen or what is right in front of us. For most, mirrors only reflect this harsh reality. But mirrors can also be used to see afar, even into infinity, to a life beyond limitation, where you are at your best, and your talents, gifts, and abilities are put to their highest and best use. Your body is filled with light and love. You are endlessly creative. And the returns on your investments flow unto you and yours continuously.

This is the ultimate payoff! You experience life without limitation: the best and highest order of you. Whole health and wealth that flows from the center, from the inside out, manifesting in your body and soul, giving you strength and power to be your best and do your best work. The big payoff is that you live in harmony with Mother Nature and stand the tough test of Father Time. In other words, your progress is sustainable over time.

BECOME A "CREATOR" TODAY THE POWER BEHIND THE AFFIRMATION

When you affirm "*I Am* a Creator," you are saying to yourself, "These words suggest a personal declaration of ownership, a statement of pride and purpose that defines who *I Am* and what I stand for."

As a creator, I see life as an endless canvas, where my imagination is the brush that paints new possibilities into existence.

The concept of creation is not limited to the physical world of art, music, or literature. It also extends to the intangible world of ideas and innovation. As a creator, I embrace the power of creativity to shape and transform the world around me, while welcoming inevitable challenges.

To be a creator, I first embrace my ability to conjure something out of nothing, to breathe life into an idea and make it real. In essence, creation is the manifestation of my thoughts and feelings, which when verbalized, crystallize into tangible reality.

As an author and creator, I realize that inspiration is all around me, from the sound of birds chirping, to the smell of freshly brewed coffee, to the feel of sun on my skin. But inspiration alone is not enough; action is required to bring thoughts to fruition.

Technology has been an incredible platform to create and innovate, allowing me to leverage the power of actual and artificial intelligence to bring my ideas to life. I believe there has never been a better time to be a creator.

As a creator, *I Am* energized by the unbridled potential of my imagination. *I Am* a mere thought away from creating something that can positively impact the world around me. Being a creator is a choice, one that comes with a responsibility to be fearless and committed in transforming dreams into reality. And for me, nothing is more fulfilling than to proclaim with utmost confidence and humility that *I Am* a creator!

AFFIRMATION IN ACTION

As you affirm, I Am a creator, imagine what you will create. Visualize your creation clearly, in detail. See it and feel it as if it were present now. Sense how your creation will bless your life and benefit others. Share your idea with a loved one and commit to it. Then draft an action plan in your I Am Journal, and take a small first step toward realizing the creation.

If you have felt inspired to create, or co-create with us, can you vividly write, in clear detail, when and what you want to create on your canvas?

____

____

____

____

____

____

____

____

____

____

____

____

SUMMARY

- How well we start often determines how well we finish.
- Money is just part of the mission, a means to a greater end.
- When you are clear on your why (your motive), you are motivated by the vision to fulfill your mission.
- Life is about progression, and your creative vision drives that progression.
- Life is not limited and your progression is sustainable over time.

— CHAPTER 6 —

I AM INTENTIONAL

"Intentional living is the art of making our own choices, before others' choices make us."

— Richie Norton

DAY 2
I AM INTENTIONAL **Proactive, Patient, Industrious, Innovative, Opportunistic, Committed, Purposeful, Vision-and Mission-Driven**

WELCOME TO MONDAY

This Monday morning of Affirmation Week, you awake not by an alarm that calls you to fight fires or change tires (wage work) but by a charm that calls you to tend and cultivate your own garden—working for incentive income. When you do Wise Work, enlightened by the Sunday Sun and illuminated by the Monday Moon, you arise for a "miracle morning."

Most people trade their time to do a task for a paycheck from an employer. Hence, they have a payday, perhaps every Friday. It's a time check for work monitored by a time clock. They often gauge their worth, even worthiness, by this paycheck. Their payday is their judgment day. Their time zone is their cage and combat zone. Few people learn how to leverage their time and talent so they continue to receive residual income at night, even while they sleep. Let's call this your paynight: you make money, even when not "on the clock," because you earn some portion of the team win, profit, or sales commission.

Consider this: Rather than work two jobs, find one line of work that can supply the income of two jobs (and more). Let your talent determine your income—not your time.

We suggest that you transition your avocation to vocation and then into wealth creation so you can enjoy a real vacation. Ask: How can I make money (wealth) from what I love to do? How can I transition from supplementary income to a primary source of income?

WHAT DOES IT MEAN TO BE "INTENTIONAL"?

The word *intention* comes from the Latin word *intentio*, meaning "to stretch toward." To be intentional is to have a clear sense of direction and purpose in everything I do. Each action I take has a defined goal and an underlying motivation behind it, whether it's the development of a new habit or the breakdown of an old one. My intentionality comes from within and is reflected in my thoughts, words, and actions.

What are your intentions? Beware of good intentions only. What you only intend to do you tend only to pretend to do, not to execute with excellence.

THE INTENTIONAL AFFIRMATION IN ACTION

CORRELATION WITH COVEY'S HABIT 2: BEGIN WITH THE END IN MIND

Covey advises starting with a clear intent, with an end in mind to envision the future you want. Use your imagination to envision what you want to become and use your conscience to decide what principles will guide you. Instead of living your life by default or based on the standards or preferences of others, set a strategic vision by asking, "What am I trying to achieve?"

You might visualize in detail your own funeral. Who is there? What are they saying about you, about how you lived your life, about your relationships? What do you want them to say? How might your priorities change if you only had thirty more days to live? Start living by these priorities. Whatever is at the center of your life will be the source of your security, guidance, wisdom, and power. Your center informs your daily decisions, actions, and motivations, and your interpretation of events. Identify timeless, unchanging principles that give you the guidance and power to align your behaviors with your beliefs and values.

Dan: A few years ago, I was doing a podcast series called *The Greatest Salesman in the World* on behalf of the Og Mandino company. As the ambassador for the company, I chose people who exhibited the amazing qualities found in this book and, in some cases, achieved extreme financial well-being. When I interviewed Thomas Kogler, a unique high achiever from Austria, he introduced me to an African mantra or proverb he uses for his team members who sell skin care and anti-aging products in Europe. When he taught me the principle behind the proverb it resonated with me. He said: "*UBUNTU* means that *I Am* because of you, and you are because of me." It hit me so strong that I paused and had him repeat it.

Then I was invited to speak at the 2023 ANMP (Association of Network Marketing Professionals) Convention to honor the life of my dear friend Nathan Ricks who tragically passed on January 2, 2023 in a plane crash. Each year, as special people pass on from this life, the director Garrett McGrath invites those close to the deceased to share a message that honors their life.

One of the amazing speakers this year flew to Dallas from Africa to share her story of how direct selling has blessed her life. Vivian Mokome took the stage and with quiet confidence shared how the spirit of UBUNTU impacts her team. When she taught the proverb UBUNTU, it reminded me of how powerful it is to say *I Am* because of you. With our team, perhaps we all can recognize and make a greater contribution to the world with this magical word, *UBUNTU*.

SPOTLIGHT: CRYSTAL BEAZER

Crystal is a mother of three children. Her background was high-level athletics, basketball in high school and junior college. But then, things sort of went haywire. "In November 2017," she said, "I had brain surgery. I had a neurologist and had brain scans done. There were no alarming signs to be seen, except what we were specifically treating."

Fast-forward to the spring of 2018. Crystal started to experience some hearing loss. "In our family, we seldom go to doctors because we take nutritious supplements. But since this hearing loss continued for a couple of weeks, I decided to go to the doctor. I was told, 'Take Sudafed, and you'll be fine.' I told him I wasn't congested, and I hadn't been sick. Anyway, I took Sudafed for two days, and then had this feeling I should go to an ENT. He was very blunt. He did tests and told me my ear was dead, I had no hearing out of that ear. He advised getting an MRI of my ear and brain to rule out tumors. So, I did the scans, and they found no tumors, but they saw lesions that could mean MS. They wanted me to do further testing. I didn't feel like I had MS, so I didn't act right away—I just put it to the side."

By the end of September 2018, Crystal felt very fatigued. "I didn't have my usual energy, and I had immense brain fog. It was hard to think, hard to be with people talking."

In October, her other ear had diminished hearing. "I knew immediately that I needed to go to the ENT. Because I acted quickly, I got steroid injections in my ear drum and oral steroids, three times in one week. That brought the hearing back in that ear, and I was so grateful. They were very concerned and wanted me to go to University of California Health (UCH)."

The first day Crystal was admitted was very intensive—a lumbar puncture, IV medications, and a two-hour MRI. "After a weeklong stay, I left with the diagnosis of MS. They said nothing else should happen until I received the MS medications, but if it did to go back to the ER."

One day later, Crystal noticed some vision loss. "I went back to the ER and sat there with my sister for *eight hours!* Every fifteen to thirty minutes, I would say a prayer: 'They told me nothing else would happen to me. I don't know what they're going to do now. Please send someone who knows what to do with me or knows what protocols to follow.' Eight hours later, a resident eye doctor looked at my eyes, looked at my past charts, and said, 'I don't think you have MS; I think you have something called Susac Syndrome.'"

Susac Syndrome is an autoimmune disease concerned with the small blood vessels in your ears, eyes, and brain. "I was told I could lose my sight and my hearing and have brain fog forever. I'd go on the Facebook support group and see people who were in bad shape. Since I was experiencing what they were and seeing worst-case scenarios, I had to keep my mindset in a positive space. Many people are misdiagnosed, given the wrong treatments, and doing the wrong things. I felt grateful that I was diagnosed correctly."

At that moment, said Crystal, "I was so grateful for that doctor. I later learned he was a member of our church. I feel that the spirit helped him to recall something he'd learned for five minutes in med school, something he could use to help me."

Crystal stayed in the hospital for another week having additional tests and taking different medicines to help the flare in her eye. "They connected me with a doctor at the hospital's eye clinic. That doctor had done his fellowship at the *only* Susac clinic in the world (only 500 people in the world have Susac Syndrome). I was amazed I was placed in such remarkable hands."

Those two hospital stays were tortuous for Crystal, and they were followed by a year of constant treatments and doctor visits. "I was putting all my energy and focus—literally everything I had—into trying to get better. I was on high-dose steroids for a long time, which is never good. For two months,

I was on an immune-suppressant infusion and pill, and IVIG (Intravenous Immunoglobulin) infusions. As of January 2023, I'm off of all that, and so I like to affirm '*I Am* healed' because the whisperings of the Spirit told me I would be healed."

For months, there was quiet downtime, a lot of solitude. "From the first hospital stay, I was wearing headphones to hear positive affirmations of healing," said Crystal. "Growing up, I was taught positivity, and I knew I had two choices: 1) I could go into a downward spiral, looking at the worst-case scenario; or 2) take my situation and use it for learning and make the best out of it by helping other people. That's why I intentionally fill my mind with positive things and choose to be close to God.

"My hope was that I would be healed, but my intentional affirmation '*I Am* healed' gave me the peace and strength that I could get through anything. I followed the doctors and listened to what they said, and I also prayed and studied scripture to know what treatment to do."

Ultimately, Crystal said, "I felt like God was the orchestrator of it all. I would take the information—from the doctors, and the holistic information—and I'd pray: 'This is the scenario; what do I do next? Do I take this medication?' And I would get answers. My faith in the power of prayer gave me hope, peace, and strength."

Now Crystal has a daily routine that she follows to attract healing, love, and patience. "On the wall in my closet are uplifting quotes and pictures of the Savior and other things. I affirm: I can make ordinary spaces, sacred spaces. I couldn't get out of bed for a long time. So, I would read and listen to uplifting messages and repeat affirmations. I needed to convince myself that I had hope for a better future."

Here are some of the affirmations that helped Crystal:

I Am calm and centered.
I Am grateful for another day to live.
I have an abundance of energy,
My body is healthy and whole.
Perfect health exists in my body.
Every day in every way I get better and better.
Something wonderful is about to happen to me.
I Am focused.
I attract positivity.
My mind and body continue to get stronger every day.
I Am letting go of fear and worry.

Crystal's condition continued through 2018 and 2019. By the end of 2019, the scans started to become clear, and they have stayed that way ever since. "I think the hardest part was being in such a condition that I couldn't recognize the person I knew I was. It was so hard not to be that person who loved to be around people, to be active, because I just couldn't. It was also hard to be doing everything in my power to get better, and then have a relapse scan."

This situation impacted Crystal as a mother as well. "I have three children, and we start our day with I Am statements and affirmations. Every morning, we say:

I Am a child of God. He knows me and loves me. With him I can do all things.
I Am strong. *I Am* brave. *I Am* beautiful. *I Am* kind.

"Then I ask each child, 'Are you going to have a good day today?'

"And they reply, 'Yes! Because I choose to have a good day.'

"I think about others who are on the path of healing, going through something equally traumatic or difficult, and I hope and pray they can fill their minds with positive affirmations and with a belief in a Higher Power."

THE LIFE-CHANGING BENEFITS OF AFFIRMING "I AM INTENTIONAL"

GO FROM COLD TO GOLD

We invite you to exit from the cold of unemployment, underemployment, and unwanted employment, and discover the gold of wise work so you can proactively create your future.

You might have bad habits that waste your time and drain your cash (gambling, addictions, and compulsions). If you don't eliminate the waste, even when you acquire wealth, you won't be able to use it optimally. Indeed, your wealth becomes slippery. So, the best way to achieve economic security is to intentionally create opportunity, to personally own your future and create a business asset that can compensate you and your heirs on a residual basis.

BECOME "INTENTIONAL" TODAY

THE POWER BEHIND THE AFFIRMATION

When you affirm "*I Am* Intentional," you are saying to yourself:

I Am more intentional than ever before. I recognize that the key to success and fulfillment is to be intentional in every aspect of my life. This means being purposeful in my relationships, work, goals, health, and happiness. In order to achieve my desired outcomes, I must be fully committed to my intentions and take steps each day toward achieving them.

In the past, I may have acted on impulse or let external circumstances dictate my direction in life. I now recognize that these actions may have kept me from realizing my full potential. By being intentional, I take ownership of my thoughts and my actions, which allows me to create the life I truly desire.

Through my increased intentionality, I can make significant changes in my life. *I Am* better able to manage my time and to achieve my goals faster. My communication with others is improving, and *I Am* creating deeper, more meaningful connections with those around me. My health and well-being are also improving as I focus on nourishing my body and mind with the things that bring me joy and fulfillment.

I Am intentional because I see the importance of living a purpose-driven life. I know my intentions guide everything I do. By focusing on what truly matters to me, *I Am* creating a life full of joy, abundance, and inner peace.

My higher level of intentionality allows me to live a life gifted to me with a sense of direction, purposefulness, and fulfillment.

AFFIRMATION IN ACTION

As you affirm, *I Am* intentional, align your vision and mission with what you intend to create or to perform and record in your *I Am* Journal how you will be proactive to see your intention come to fruition.

____

____

____

____

____

____

____

____

SUMMARY

- The key to success and fulfillment is to be intentional in every aspect of your life.
- Be intentional by having a clear sense of direction and purpose in everything you do.
- UBUNTU: I Am because of you, and you are because of me.
- I will have a good day today because I choose to have a good day.

— CHAPTER 7 —

I AM PRESENT

"Practice sharing the fullness of your being, your best self, your enthusiasm, your vitality, your spirit, your trust, your openness, above all, your presence. Share it with yourself, with your family, with the world."

— Jon Kabat-Zinn

DAY 3
I AM PRESENT **Focused, Prescient, Positive, Enlightened, Alert, Aware, Alive, Empathic, Considerate, Optimistic, Filled with Hope and Faith**

WELCOME TO TUESDAY

Today is Tuesday, named after Tiu, the Germanic God of War. In Romance languages, it is named for Mars, the Greek God of War. So, today, the Tuesday of Affirmation Week, we declare war—on *stasis*, low energy, sameness, ruts and routines, resignation, angst, and apathy. Tuesday is a day of energy and growth.

Your mission to Mars is fueled by energy, visions, and dreams. Your motive in this mission to Mars is to get the red out (out of debt). It's a mission to break bad habits (physical, mental, and emotional) that keep you bound by inertia. Yes, any journey of a thousand miles begins with a first step, but your first step may be your last unless you have a strategy whereby you secure competitive advantage via innovation and the wise management of talent and energy.

Let your purpose fuel your passion. Tuesday is a day to invest your positive energy in the areas of your strength, purpose, passion, or cause—preferably in the company of others who are likewise invested and share your dream.

WHAT DOES IT MEAN TO BE "PRESENT"?

The word *present* comes from the Latin word *praesent*, meaning "at hand" or "in front of." To be present means to be fully engaged and focused on the current moment, rather than dwelling on the past or worrying about the future. Being present is a state of mind that requires us to be fully aware of our surroundings, thoughts, and emotions, without judgment.

Being present is critical to our wellbeing and happiness. When we are present, we can fully appreciate and experience the simple joys of life that we might otherwise miss. We can connect more deeply with ourselves and others, creating richer and more meaningful relationships. Being present can also reduce anxiety and stress, as we learn to let go of worries and focus on the here and now.

To help stay present, practice mindfulness. Take time each day to focus on breathing and to tune in to feelings and emotions. Recognize that thoughts come and go, so try not to attach too strongly to them. Instead, seek to maintain an open mind and stay grounded in the present moment.

Being fully engaged in the present moment requires us to put aside distractions and experience the notions, emotions, and sensations in the moment. It also means being attentive in conversation while letting go of judgment and preconceived notions about the other person.

Being present is an affirmation of being alive, of living our lives fully and with clarity. As we become more present, we train our brains to be focused, clear, and attuned to the world around us. With practice, being fully engaged in the present moment comes naturally and helps us find lasting fulfillment in everything we do.

THE PRESENT AFFIRMATION IN ACTION

Dan: Recently I interviewed Kimberly Wilkerson, the founder of Token Clothing Company, and she shared her *I Am* experience. Desiring to positively impact women through fashion, she decided to make clothes with *I Am* statements in them. She involved a small study group and identified the three statements that most resonated with them: *I Am* loved, *I Am* worthy, and *I Am* beautiful. She imprinted these *I Am* statements on the interior of the fabric with an option to turn the top inside out so that the words would rest against your skin while you sleep. The *I Am* statements are also printed forward and backward, enabling wearers to read them in the mirror (if they turn the top inside out) and another person could read them when talking to or looking at the wearer of the clothing. This is another outstanding example of how we can all choose the words and affirmations we use to be present and build the house we live in.

But being present can be a challenge, particularly in today's world. We are constantly bombarded by distractions and endless to-do lists. We multitask, moving from one thing to the next without fully engaging in any of them. It takes effort and practice to remain present, but it is a skill that can be learned and honed.

One effective way to cultivate presence and become more positive and prescient is through mindfulness practices such as meditation. By sitting quietly and focusing on the present moment, we train our minds to stay present in our daily lives. Also, we might set aside time each day to disconnect from technology and other distractions and devote our attention to the present moment.

Being present is a powerful tool for creating meaningful connections, managing stress, and fully experiencing life. It's easy to get caught up in the past or future, but the beauty and richness of life lie in the moments we experience now. By taking time to cultivate presence in our lives, we can live with greater intention, joy, and peace. Being present (listening with empathy) is the greatest "present" (gift) we can give other people.

CORRELATION WITH COVEY'S HABIT 3: PUT FIRST THINGS FIRST

You put first things first when you are present and prioritize what's important over what's urgent. You execute your priorities, not simply react to urgent matters. You spend time doing the most important things, not simply managing crises, problems, and other people.

We tend to spend most of our time reacting to matters that seem urgent when their perceived urgency is often based on others' priorities and expectations. This leads to short-term focus, feeling out of control, and having shallow or broken relationships.

The Eisenhower Matrix describes four categories of Urgent/Important. Quadrant II (important but not urgent) deals with things like building relationships, long-term planning, exercising, preparation—things that don't feel urgent. To focus our time on Quadrant II, we have to learn how to say "no" to other activities that seem urgent and delegate effectively. We're thinking ahead, working on the roots, and preventing crises from happening in the first place! We maintain a primary focus on relationships and results, and a secondary focus on time and making a dime. We focus on effectiveness with people and efficiency with things.

SPOTLIGHT: AMANDA EARNEST

Oddly enough, Amanda's thirst for personal development came, she said, "from feeling like a big, fat loser." She once thought only weird people shopped in the personal development section of the bookstore or attended Tony Robbins events.

"I've been fortunate to have loving mentors who were brave enough to tell me how it really was. I believe it was because I had self-esteem and a sense of self-worth that caused me to think, 'I've got this. I've gone to college.' I was reminded I needed a software update! I was told: Becoming the person you want to be, accomplishing the things you want to do, and having the things you want to have will require more of you.

"After two years of being stubborn and wanting to do things my way, I figured out that I didn't know what I didn't know. I was able to shift that and learn more about myself—what was right and wrong. The more I learned, the more I realized how much I had yet to learn. I realized it was time for me to follow the money. That doesn't necessarily mean follow the financial success of other people, but success leaves clues. The world pays you what you're worth."

Amanda came to this conclusion: "I realized that the people who were having a big impact—which is what I wanted to do—naturally became wealthy. I started looking and noticing the clues. A common denominator was that they were following a mighty quest to become a better person."

She realized that version 1.0 of her had a self-esteem that was almost arrogance, and that was hurting her. "I looked at it as, I don't need to do all this work; it's so hard, such a waste of time. But as I grew, I developed a self-esteem that came from a more humble place. It evolved from this idea: Because I have self-esteem and because *I Am* worthy, I must do these things in order to help other people come around to this as well."

Three affirmations shaped her life: *I Am* present, *I Am* prioritizing, and *I Am* serving. And the one that supersedes all others is one she was taught as a girl: *I Am* a Child of God.

"A few years into my business," she reports, "I was spread thin and had a paralyzing sense of obligation to every area of my life. It seemed no matter what I was doing, I was always letting another area of my life down. I'd think that my family wasn't getting what they needed, that I wasn't being a good mom. These stories (negative affirmations) played over and over in my head. If my phone pinged while I was with my family, I felt I was a bad leader. Wherever I was, I wasn't good enough. Where my feet were at the moment meant I wasn't in the five other places I needed to be."

That is when Amanda experienced a life-changing shift. "When I stopped looking to all the other places I felt I needed to be and started to look down at my feet, take a deep breath, and observe where my feet were at that moment, I was able to be fully present there. I went from a place of feeling ragged, spread thin, and not measuring up in any area to understanding the difference between the noun *balance* and the verb *balancing*—moving between areas of our lives with intention and joyful purpose."

For example, Amanda says, "While I was driving kids, I'd always have an AirPod in my ear, even if I wasn't listening to anything. Maybe we can walk and chew gum at the same time, but we may miss many meaningful things—like being present with our children, even on a short car ride. Or we could be sending a message to someone or listening to an audio book. It goes in one ear and out the other. We think we're multitasking, but I call it nothing-tasking."

So, she said, "I started to take the AirPod out. Even if my son or daughter didn't have anything to say, I was holding space, being quiet, and being available for them at that moment. Instead of feeling bad and thinking, *I'm not*, or thinking about everything what I wasn't doing, I began to feel grateful, proud, and excited about what *I Am* currently doing. This changed everything for me."

She now affirms: *I Am* present because *I Am* prioritizing. "While my life's priorities remain relatively constant, my current priority may not be my number-one thing. For example, I would say God is my number-one priority, but I don't have to set up a tent inside the church and live there. It's okay to move between those priorities, dynamically, energetically with joy. *I Am* fully fired up and stoked out of my mind to be where *I Am* right now."

Amanda reports making a positive impact on youth with *I Am* statements. "One of the best things we can do for kids is to teach them who they are: they are loved, they are worthy, they are valuable, capable, and beautiful; they are children of God. It's rough out there. They deal with a lot, and reinforcing who they are, at their core, empowers them to handle challenges."

She also affirms: *I Am* serving. "Service is a cool way to find joy in life. I appreciate the importance of taking care of myself—putting on the oxygen mask first before I assist others—but I sense the culture of self-care and 'me time' is getting out of hand. Many depressed people take good care of themselves and have a lot of 'me time.'"

Some of the happiest, most fulfilling experiences in her life, Amanda says, are not sitting at a day spa, as lovely as that is! "If you ask 100 people, most will tell you of an experience where they connected with others, perhaps as a volunteer to build houses, go on a church mission, visit their kid's school, or whatever makes them happy—outside of themselves—in a service-oriented capacity. Service is such a powerful way to experience a joyful life.

"*I Am* serving is a great affirmation for me. For instance, if I'm picking up dirty laundry, I may feel irritated; but if I affirm—*I Am* serving my family by doing the laundry—then I no longer see it as an obnoxious chore. I'm serving my family today. I'm serving my team by doing our team recognition post. So, look at everything and ask yourself, *Am I* serving right now?

"I think that life can be a blast. You can find joy and fulfillment outside of yourself as well as having the positive impact and influence that you want to have."

Amanda also affirms: Get over yourself. "Someone once said that to me when I was new in this business. I was nervous, self-absorbed, feeling more people were judging me than even noticing me. I needed a reminder to get over myself, to know that I could grow, divest of arrogance and pride, and have grace with myself."

Success leaves us with these clues for a reason, she says. "Don't hesitate to step outside your comfort zone and step inside the world of personal development. It's going to help you. There's no downside to reading a book like this. If you pay attention, you won't be stuck in the same place today as you were yesterday. I guarantee you: affirmations like this are going to stick. They are going to have a positive effect. So, be one of those weird people who shops in the personal development section of the bookstore! Don't fight the feeling; just come in with us!"

HOW TO BECOME "PRESENT"

OVERCOMING APATHY AND ANGST

We all have to decide at some point in life whether to sacrifice our own dreams to support the dreams of others. It's a very sad day when we surrender our dream.

"When Dreams die, life is a broken-winged bird that cannot fly."

— Langston Hughes

On the other hand:

"Cowards die a thousand deaths;
the valiant taste of death but once."

— Shakespeare

When you start a work week with Monday's sense of futility, you naturally drift into Tuesday with apathy. Apathy is the great enemy of ambition and empathy. Apathy strangles ambition and produces angst. So, we tend to deny, defer, and delay our needs. We sink into resignation, abdication, regression, recession, and depression. Scarcity thinking leads to pain and poverty. Ambition loses out to apathy and entropy when we lack a vision, mission, or goal—or fail to tie our daily activities to a higher purpose that enables us to get through hard times and challenges. Newton's law of motion—objects at rest tend to stay at rest—prevails when we jump into something with gusto, but lazy habits pull us back into a state of stasis.

We may suffer from the effects of scar tissue. We have tried before and failed. So why try again? Self-doubt causes us to succumb to resignation or compromise.

We may be unemployed or underemployed. Nothing damages the psyche more than this sense of being unwanted or undervalued in the market and having to go it alone.

YOUR *I AM* MISSION STATEMENTS

What is your life mission? Do you have personal and professional mission statements?

When we examine the best mission statements, we find that they are all inspiring; in fact, in none of them is the purpose or intent expressed in terms of maximizing revenue or profit or beating competitors. This is not how those who truly create wealth express their intent.

Any worthy mission must be put into action by executing principles and practices (daily disciplines that lead to desired results). The result is the creation of wealth. And when this formula is put into action on a large scale, the result is the creation of energy.

Energy drives prosperity. And Whole Wealth is much more of a marathon than a sprint. Therefore, any extra weight adds to the coefficient of drag (physics). Of course, drag or extra weight is often self-inflicted—it can include any resistance or interference that we inflict on ourselves—such as poor financial decisions or negative, cynical, or sarcastic self-talk.

Negative self-talk can seriously deplete our energy, destroy our self-confidence, make us feel worthless, and cause a poor self-image and identity. Negative self-talk can also be created by certain others around us who are dream-stealers. They are the first to tell us we are crazy for pursuing our dreams. They are the cynics, skeptics, and contrarians who rain on our parade.

Do all you can to avoid dream-stealers! If you can't tune them out, walk away. Intense exposure to negative energy fields can drain years of positive energy affirmations. So, avoid the hazardous influence of dream-stealers. Never give up on your dreams as a result of comments from people who already gave up on theirs.

THE LIFE-CHANGING BENEFITS OF AFFIRMING "I AM PRESENT"

POSITIVE MIND ENERGY

The discipline of Affirmation Week is to filter what enters your mind in order to keep the flow positive. One thing that distinguishes successful leaders is the way they think. They know intuitively that positive energy has more power than negative energy. Positive energy gives them the power and stamina to solve perplexing problems, endure trials, and finish the good things they start. They don't settle for less when they can finish the mission and have the best!

For example, Nu Skin founder Blake Roney once wrote a one-page instruction manual on how to succeed as a leader: "Great leaders are not derailed by things that they can't control; they look through the challenges, and they forge ahead with hope and optimism."

We urge you to avoid negativity because negative thoughts waste energy and can lead to entropy and keep you from being successful. Affirm your beliefs and doubt your doubts.

Ken: For many years in my presentations, I have demonstrated the Power of Positivity using a simple arm exercise. I invite a person, usually a strong man, to stand next to me and extend his right or left arm, the one he thinks is stronger.

I then proceed to be critical of him and to project my view of his weaknesses, faults, failures, and shortcomings. Then I tell him to resist my efforts to push down his arm. Even when he tries his best to resist, I can usually push his arm down with just two fingers.

I then extol what I perceive to be his positive traits and strengths, his successes, talents, and powers. I ask him to imagine a divine power coming down through the crown of his head to his feet, serving as a steel beam to anchor him. And I tell him his extended arm is now connected to this higher power, making him invincible.

When I try this time to push down his arm, I must expend about 10X the energy, often using both my hands and all my strength. Lesson: Positivity has 10X the power of negativity!

BECOME "PRESENT" TODAY

THE POWER BEHIND THE AFFIRMATION

When you affirm "*I Am* Present," you are saying to yourself: *I Am* present and positive. These words hold tremendous power. They remind us we are here, in this moment, alive and breathing. It's easy to get caught up in the past, worrying about mistakes we've made, or in the future, worrying about what's to come. In truth, the only time that truly matters is right now, as these sages confirm:

"No one can lose the past or the future; no one can lose what he doesn't have. The present is the only thing one can lose."

— Marcus Aurelius

"In reality, there is only now, if you know how to handle this moment, you know how to handle eternity."

— Sadhguru

"Now is the only reality. All else is either memory or imagination."

— Osho

"Without Hope in your Future, your present loses meaning."

— Benjamin Hardy

YOUR POSITIVE PICTURE OF PROSPERITY

You are born for a purpose—to progress and prosper. You progress step by step, day by day, from one milestone to the next. Nothing gives you energy like a sense of progress toward your picture of prosperity. It's why we have milestones on the path to becoming a sales leader, and upon achieving each milestone we celebrate success.

Ask yourself: What is my picture of prosperity? Beyond creating a dream board—a compilation of images clipped from magazines that represent what you want to achieve in life (usually material assets and possessions)—you might picture your dream life. It should reflect what you want to be, do, and represent, not simply what you want to own and possess. It's a picture made in the present that affirms future prosperity.

AFFIRMATION IN ACTION

As part of your I Am present affirmation, you might take a Progress Photo on each of the seven days of affirmation and finish your week with a Photo Finish—your completion of Affirmation Week in your on-going quest for whole health and wealth.

You might share your photos on Facebook, in your I Am Journal, or on our website at www.AffirmIAm.com. One purpose of this book is to create an I Am Affirmation Community or social network and enterprise that enable us to see other faces and pictures to sustain our progress.

SUMMARY

- Cultivate being present through mindfulness practices such as meditation.
- I Am present, I Am prioritizing, I Am serving, and I Am a Child of God.
- Be one of those weird people who shops in the personal development section of the bookstore!
- Avoid negativity. Affirm your beliefs and doubt your doubts.
- Create your picture of progress and prosperity.

SECTION III

WIN THE DAY
Character and Competence

In this section, we make three more affirmations to win the day: *I Am* worthy, *I Am* capable, and *I Am* compassionate.

AFFIRMATION 4: *I Am* Worthy.

AFFIRMATION 5: *I Am* Capable.

AFFIRMATION 6: *I Am* Compassionate.

— CHAPTER 8 —

I AM WORTHY

"Love yourself first and everything else falls into line. You really have to love yourself to get anything done in this world."

— Lucille Ball

DAY 4
I AM WORTHY **Deserving, Favored, Chosen, Blessed, Abundant, Unique, Grateful, Prayerful, Clean, Wise, Servant, Friend, Provider, Protector, Missionary, Child of God**

WELCOME TO WEDNESDAY

Wednesday is named for the Norse God Woden or Odin. In Romance languages, though, it is named for the Roman god Mercury. He is the god of commerce and travel and the Roman counterpart of the Greek god Hermes, the swift messenger. All three gods were messenger gods who could move swiftly. (The planet Mercury received its name because it moves quickly across the sky.)

And so, on this day, the key word is action—to make a move, motion, or proposal. Being proactive suggests that you choose your response to conditions and conditioning. You become a pioneer, pilgrim, or trailblazer. You leave the land of security and familiarity to venture into your own opportunity, but not alone. You recruit a team and lead. You rely on your wits—and on each other—rather than trust in false guarantees, warrantees, and securities. You see that real security lies in your resourcefulness, not your resources.

To overcome homeostasis, we need to seek opportunity, commit to change, develop a support system, and follow a regular practice of making affirmations, including *I Am* worthy!

THE WORTHY AFFIRMATION IN ACTION

Ken: Once I was driving home after a book I had been editing was rejected by the publisher. Needless to say, I was feeling down. I refer to such situations as the circus of defamation and rejection in opposition to the circle of affirmation and acceptance.

Since I hadn't eaten before my "Zoom and Doom" meeting with the publisher, I was hungry and stopped at one of my favorite fast-food restaurants, Arctic Circle, "where the good stuff is."

I ordered the All-American comfort food meal: cheeseburger, French fries, chocolate shake, and root beer. After taking a few bites, I reached for the drink and noticed the cup. I couldn't believe my eyes! I was reading positive affirmations: *You are worthy, loved, helpful, resilient, beautiful, capable, valuable, brave, strong, talented, inspiring, amazing, unique, enough!* Suddenly, I left the Circle of Defamation and slipped back inside the Circle of Affirmation, the all-inclusive circle of acceptance, inside the Arctic Circle.

And here's the amazing rest of the story: I started to see the rejection as a blessing in disguise, not as failure but as a welcome closure, a chance to make a fresh start. Seconds earlier, it seemed like a door had been slammed in my face—now I saw a window of greater opportunity opening before me.

Everywhere you and I go—every turn we take, every transaction we make, and with everybody we meet—we receive "You Are" messages: "You are this" and "You are that," based on people's perceptions, impressions, or evaluations of you, which may be formed even before you ever meet in person and may be based mostly on biases, prejudices, and stereotypes.

Ironically, if we constantly react to "you are" messages, we may never know who we are because often these "You Are" messages are mixed or ambiguous if not downright negative.

Indeed, in the course of any given day, we may receive such negative "You Are" messages as: "You are incompetent, stupid, wrong, weak, ugly...a loser, a failure, an idiot."

This is why *I Am* affirmations must be stronger than *You Are* defamations. We decide who we are; we define who we are; we show who we are by our thoughts and actions, our works and desires, our character and competence. And it helps if we belong to a circle of acceptance—a society of family, friends, associates, neighbors, club or church members.

Many people forfeit wealth because they don't feel worthy due to low self-worth.

CORRELATION WITH COVEY'S HABIT 4: THINK WIN-WIN OR NO DEAL

If you don't feel worthy of your win, you won't seek and attain Win-Win outcomes. Covey notes that Win-Win situations are mutually beneficial and satisfying to each party. There are six possible outcomes in interactions:

1. *Win-Win*: Both people win. Agreements or solutions are mutually beneficial and satisfying.
2. *Win-Lose*: If I win, you lose. Win-Lose people are prone to use position, power, credentials, and personality to get their way.
3. *Lose-Win*: I lose, you win. Lose-Win people are quick to please and appease and seek strength from popularity or acceptance.
4. *Lose-Lose*: Both people lose. When two Win-Lose people get together—that is, when two determined, stubborn, ego-invested individuals interact—the result will be Lose-Lose.
5. *Win*: Winners seek to get what they want, even at the expense of others.
6. *Win-Win or No Deal*: Without a mutually beneficial agreement, there is no deal.

The "No Deal" option liberates us from needing to manipulate people and push our own agenda. We can be open and understand the underlying issues. Win-Win requires consideration, courage, and an abundance mentality—a belief that there's plenty out there for everyone.

The scarcity mentality suggests that everything is zero-sum (if you get it, I don't). People with this mindset have a hard time sharing recognition or credit and being genuinely happy about other people's successes. The more we practice Win-Win, the more powerful our influence.

SPOTLIGHT: CHRISTIANA BURTON

Christiana shares her story with anyone who has ever doubted themselves, felt unworthy, or been in deep despair. "I'll tell you how it was for me—and about the power of faith and overcoming things you never thought you could."

Christiana was born in Knoxville, Tennessee, and had a rough childhood since her mom abused drugs. "When I was four years old, she went to prison. My twin brother and I bounced back and forth from our father to our grandmother. She had a strong Christian faith, and I attribute much of the good in my life to her and her influence. Also, my dad was abusive; and when we were with him, we didn't know if we would have food on the table, or even if we'd have a toothbrush."

When Christiana was eight years old, her mom got out of prison, but she didn't live with her mom until she was twelve. "We moved to the projects, the ghetto, and started skipping school and doing all the things kids shouldn't do. My mom got pregnant again, but not by my father."

Christiana was in the ninth grade when she moved from Tennessee to Kentucky. "I loved sports, track, and cross-country, but anyone who's into sports knows you've got to be in the game. We were moving so much—I went to three different high schools—so I couldn't stay on the team. In tenth grade I met Joe, my high school sweetheart. I was only fourteen, but Joe was a breath of fresh air. He helped me escape many bad situations. He was my protector."

At fifteen, Christiana started working, first at McDonald's and then Target, and decided to drop out of school. "I regret it now and don't recommend doing what I did, but I was so wrapped up with Joe and wanted a new and different life. One day I talked with my tenth grade English teacher, Mr. Dixon, about dropping out. He said, 'You haven't even started senior year. If you drop out of school, no college will accept you—you'll never make anything out of your life.'

"I told him that he was wrong. 'You'll see,' I said. Everyone thought I was dropping out because I was pregnant, but that wasn't it at all. I took courses and got my GED. Then, at sixteen, I enrolled in a community technical college in Kentucky. I was still living at home when I decided I wanted to be a nurse, but Joe decided he wanted to move to Florida, so I went along. His mother also came along. If I could have seen the road ahead, I don't know if I would have gone with him. I thought about running off without telling my mother, but I decided I should talk with her. Since I was then seventeen, she threatened to call the police but never did."

In Florida, Christiana worked at a frozen yogurt shop and at IHOP. "I was still in nursing school when Joe started having problems with his hip. He had multiple surgeries and couldn't work. So, we decided to get married! I was now eighteen, but not old enough to drink alcohol on my honeymoon. It seemed I was always working and taking care of everyone else, including Joe. Since I love kids, I next decided to become a teacher. I taught elementary school for several years. Joe continued to have orthopedic issues; at age twenty-five, he underwent a total hip replacement. He was in so much pain and started taking painkillers—hardcore medication. Because of my childhood, I was supersensitive to drug abuse, and honestly, I didn't want to be around it, but I honored my wedding vows—*for better or worse*—I loved my husband."

In her mind, Christiana thought Joe would get better. "But things only got worse. Joe was diagnosed with ankylosing spondylitis, a life-threatening autoimmune disease that causes bones in the spine to fuse and can cause a hunched posture and difficulty breathing. The drug he was on was powerful, one side effect being possible blindness. Needless to say, Joe was severely depressed and was judged by people for not working. Since I was his caregiver, I had to do everything from bathing him to changing his bedpan while teaching and working at IHOP."

Then Joe's mom was diagnosed with a brain tumor, glioblastoma. It affected her speech and vision. She didn't know where she was or even know her name. An oncologist said she had six months to live.

"Even at this low point," said Christiana, "I had faith that things would get better. But Joe was getting more depressed and was taking meds and drank whiskey and beer. That year, on Christmas, his mom wrote him a letter that began, 'If I should die before I wake.' This only made things worse; he was seeing a psychiatrist who put him on anxiety depression medication. But he continued to drink. He was drinking and driving recklessly."

In January 2020, Joe told his psychiatrist he was having suicidal thoughts. Two days later, Christiana received a frantic call from his mom. "Joe is suicidal!" she screamed.

"I called Joe, but he didn't pick up," says Christiana. "Finally, he called me back. He told me to tell everyone that he loved them and said to me, 'Always remember, I love you.'

"I called the cops. By the time I got to the house, it was swarming with paramedics; I had a panic attack. I remember getting out my car and heading toward the house—when I heard a gunshot from inside. I heard screaming; Joe's mom was in there. I dropped to my knees on the sidewalk. He'd killed himself. I was in a full panic now, and they took me to the hospital."

Afterward, Christiana stayed in a motel for a few days with Joe's mom. "I went to see him at the morgue so I could remember how he looked. I wrote a love letter to him, for the eulogy. And then, I went into a severe, dark, and deep depression."

Christiana took two weeks off from school and continued to take care of Joe's mom. "She blamed me for his suicide, for everything. I knew it was just her brain tumor that caused her to say what she did. Still, it was hard to hear. Two months later, she passed away; and I found myself living alone for the first time in my life, in a three-bedroom house full of furniture, seventeen hours away from my family. My mom and brother came to see me. We cleared out the furniture, and I moved into my first apartment. And I started taking medication for depression. I didn't like the way it made me feel, and so I started drinking to numb the pain."

At this dark time, Christiana scrolled through Facebook and found a direct sales opportunity. "I definitely needed to make more money. I didn't get a single penny from Joe or his mother. But so much more than money I needed the community, the women. I had nobody."

That was when Christiana met Jesse, her Chapter 2. "I was fishing—that's how we met. He was right there like a shining light on the side of the Intracoastal. I laid out my whole story.

He'd moved from New York. Neither of us knew anyone. We became good friends."

In the fall of 2020, Christiana wanted a whole new life. "I wasn't financially stable enough to stop teaching, but I told my principal that I wanted to go full time in direct sales. It only took me six months to achieve the highest level in the pay plan! I stopped taking all the medications; my drinking slowed down. Now, I have friends, I exercise. My entire life has changed. *I Am* pregnant with my first child, and I bought a home. I'm the first in my family to own a home."

Christiana reflects: "Many people told me I wasn't worthy, and that has been fuel for the fire. I became part of a community that led me to reading, to learning about affirmations and positive self-talk. I now have a daily Miracle Morning routine, and that has made a huge difference! Before, I was working hard, but I kept hitting a wall. It was forced, and not fun."

Now, Christiana has read many books, and they have helped her in all aspects of her life. "I've learned my past doesn't define me. I'm not proud of my past, but it made me stronger. I know I can handle anything. I've also learned that *I Am* worthy of all the good things that come my way. My mother-in-law, my high school teacher, and many others made me feel I wasn't worthy. I was angry with God after Joe died. After I got past the anger, I brought faith back into my life. I pray for others and their well-being; the more people you can help the better!"

Christiana's daily devotionals keep her faith strong. "I believe that faith and hard work go hand in hand. You can have all the faith in the world, but you've got to put in the work; and you can work all you want, but you've got to have faith."

One of her favorite books is *The High 5 Habit* by Mel Robbins. "I give myself a high-five every morning. It's not possible to give yourself a high-five and start the day sour. And I have learned, despite what Mr. Dixon and my mother-in-law said, and despite all the odds and hardship and all the struggles, that *I Am* worthy!"

BECOME "WORTHY TODAY"

THE POWER BEHIND THE AFFIRMATION

When you affirm, "*I Am* Worthy," you are saying to yourself that: *I Am* worthy and deserving of all the love, happiness, and success the Universe has to offer. I trust in my power to manifest my dreams and attract positivity into my life. I deeply believe in my ability to create my own reality, and I know I deserve the best life has to offer.

I release all negative thoughts and beliefs that hold me back from achieving my goals. I focus on my strengths and talents, and I believe *I Am* capable of overcoming the obstacles that come my way. *I Am* worthy of success, and *I Am* deserving of praise.

I trust in the Universe's plan for me. When faced with challenges or setbacks, I see them as steppingstones on my journey toward greater success and fulfillment. *I Am* strong, confident, and full of limitless potential.

I deeply appreciate all of the blessings and opportunities that come my way, and I express gratitude for them every day. *I Am* open to receiving abundance in all forms, and I trust that as long as I stay true to myself and my dreams, all of my heart's desires will come to fruition.

I Am worthy and deserving of a happy and fulfilling life, and I fully embrace my power to create it. Daily I take actionable steps toward my goals with confidence and determination. *I Am* a force to be reckoned with, and *I Am* ready to see and seize every good opportunity that comes my way.

Affirming my worthiness and deservingness every day brings me closer to achieving my dreams and living the life I desire and deserve. *I Am* infinitely capable, and I trust in my own power to manifest my deepest desires with ease and grace.

If you sense a gap between the affirmation of your worth or your worthiness, consider the case of Christiana Burton.

AFFIRMATION IN ACTION

When you make the affirmation *I Am* worthy, you might recall a time or two in recent days when you did something noteworthy or praiseworthy and record this story in your *I Am* Journal. Reflect on your talents and strengths, your good traits and deeds, and seek to replicate them in order to reinforce your sense of personal worthiness. By doing this daily, a weakness may become a strength, and a flaw, sin, or mistake be corrected.

SUMMARY

- If you don't feel worthy of your win, you won't seek and attain Win-Win outcomes.
- Faith and hard work go hand in hand.

- Give yourself a high-five every day. You can't feel sour when you high-five.
- *I Am* Worthy. I deeply believe in my ability to create my own reality, and I know I deserve the best life has to offer.

— CHAPTER 9 —

I AM CAPABLE

"If you plan on being anything less than you are capable of being, you will probably be unhappy all the days of your life."

— Abraham Maslow

DAY 5
I AM CAPABLE **Qualified, Competent, Prepared, Confident, Strong, Powerful, Intelligent, Coach, Teacher, Reader, Leader, Motivator, Builder, Winner, Bold, Fearless, Courageous, Gifted, Skilled**

WELCOME TO THURSDAY

Thursday is named in English after Thor, the Norse God of Thunder and Storm. In Romance languages, it's named after the Roman god Jupiter (*jeudi* in French), who is Zeus in Greek mythology. Since Storm seems to be the New Norm, we invite you to see Thursday as your day to thunder—to gain voice and visibility, to lift and gain leverage.

The best and fastest way out of the quicksand traps of Money Mythology is to gain lift and leverage—to change the ratio from one-to-one to one-to-many. Whole Wealth requires that you collaborate with a partner that frees you to do what you do best—

like network and sell—without being stymied by all the duties of starting and running a business and the constraints of traditional business models. The quest today is to find and leverage the right business partner.

How can you best leverage your time, money, resources, and talents? Since breakthroughs often require breaks with the past and old paradigms, we suggest you learn the physics of financial leadership: use levers and leverage to lift off. Leverage provides some measure of mechanical and monetary advantage.

THE CAPABLE AFFIRMATION IN ACTION

COORELATION WITH COVEY'S HABIT 6: SYNERGIZE

Synergy allows us to create new alternatives, options, and possibilities, such as one plus one equals three or more and the whole is greater than the sum of its parts. We write new scripts, leave the comfort zone, and venture into a new enterprise. We can work and reason together to create a third alternative to meet the challenges we face. By doing so, we have a transformation, not merely a transaction. Both sides get what they want, and they build their relationship. By valuing our differences, we can synthesize insights and ideas to create synergy. If two people have the same opinion, one is unnecessary. When we become aware of a different perspective, we can say, "Good! You see it differently! Help me see what you see." We find strength and utility in different perspectives in order to create new possibilities and win-win results.

Valuing the differences enables us to experience synergy, expand our perspective, avoid negative energy, see the good in others, exercise courage to be open, catalyze creativity, and find solutions that will benefit everyone by looking for a third alternative.

SPOTLIGHT: KENNY BRADY

We all put labels on ourselves, says Kenny Brady, an expert on parenting. "These labels might be intuitive or things we hear as we grow up, the way we were raised by our parents and the things they believed in. Hopefully, we learn to think positively about ourselves because others may want us to think a different way or show up a certain way. If we think about it spiritually, we are all Godlike. There's so much more to learn about who we are, who we can become, and how we can help each other."

Speaking as a parent, Kenny says he hopes to be the greatest influence on his kids while they are in the house, before they get influenced by everything around them like social media, friends, and teachers—people who may not have the same beliefs, hopes, and dreams he has for them. "Growing up, we had early morning seminary, and that had a profound impact on me as a teenager. Not only did it set a tone for the spiritual foundation for my day, but it put me with those who believed the same things."

So, Kenny wondered, how could he start that earlier in life? "I started with my daughter Lola when she was thirteen, a teenager in her prime years of development. When I had time with her in the morning, I would talk with her and say funny things. I have four kids now, and I'm in the car with them for an hour every morning, driving to three different schools. I wondered, *What can I do to bless them during this precious one-on-one time? How can I influence them? What might be like an early morning seminary where we set a foundation for the day and encourage belief and gratitude—something that becomes a habit?"*

Kenny started what he called ***Stop Sign Affirmations***. "When I was a teenager, my dad and I played a game called Slug Bugs to pass the time on the road. We'd see an old Volkswagen Beetle and we'd yell out, 'Slug Bug!' and then punch each other in the arm. On the way to school, we'd see ten to fifteen slug bugs. It became a fun thing."

Remembering that time with his dad, Kenny wanted to have something like that with his kids. "When driving to school, we encountered seven stop signs. When we approached a stop sign, we would brake to stop the car for a few seconds—time enough for a short affirmation!"

The first stop sign was just three houses down, and the first affirmation is a belief in the great *I Am*: I have faith in the Lord Jesus Christ. "Christ is the one who said *I Am*. He talked about '*I Am* the good shepherd' and '*I Am* the way, the truth, and the life.' So, the affirmation at the first stop sign sets the tone for the other stop signs. All my kids—my four-year-old, my nine-year-old, my eleven-year-old, and my thirteen-year-old—we all say: 'I have faith in Jesus Christ.'"

At the second stop sign, the affirmation is *I Am* confident. "This affirmation plants the seeds of confidence in who they are, on top of their faith in Christ. Sometimes, they affirm: *I Am* kind, or *I Am* love, or *I Am* safe. Sometimes, we'll quote Og Mandino: 'I greet this day with love in my heart!' Or they'll say, *I Am* a Brady—our family name, meaning *I Am* capable. I Can Do Hard Things. Or *I Am* grateful. Thank you!

Kenny hopes these *I Am* affirmations are powerful for his children because "they're going to get out of the car and be with their friends who have different influences, beliefs, thoughts, and ideas. And in their classes, their teachers may teach them different concepts. I want them to have faith and trust in who they are. I want them to know they can be lights to others."

Some days, making affirmations is not easy, says Kenny. "They might say, 'I don't want to do this one,' or they say, *I Am*—whatever without much enthusiasm. But we do this every day. My four-year-old is kind of quiet, and every now and then, she'll say, 'I'm confident. Dad, did you hear me?'

"We do this every morning," continues Kenny. "When we see any stop sign, wherever we are, they'll say: Stop Sign—something. Sometimes, I'll have my nieces or nephews with us, and they'll ask what we're doing, and we get a chance to talk about stop sign affirmations."

"Affirmations are powerful because they're our self-talk," says Kenny. "What do we see and say to ourselves when we look in the mirror? What do we hear coming out of our mouth? Whatever we say resonates inside as truth, and it comes out in everything we do, whether it's positive or negative. We make sure it's the right truth about ourselves."

In business, Kenny plays a leadership role by coaching others, mostly "incredible" women. "I believe women shape our society. In working with them, I see they have the greatest influence for good in this world, yet they also have self-talk that can be positive or negative. I've seen someone change before my eyes and become who they truly are."

In his business, Kenny sells comfortable clothing that is also flattering. "It makes women feel beautiful. But sometimes they are reluctant to try something on because when they go into a dressing room and try something on, what do they do? They look in the mirror and talk to themselves subconsciously—immediately—because they want to know how it looks, how it fits. They're thinking, 'Is it comfortable? Is it flattering?'

"Now, often for the first time in their life, they'll say, *I Am* beautiful. They look good. Then, others compliment them, and maybe they haven't received a compliment in a long time.

"I tell those in leadership, you can change someone's life. They can look in the mirror and say, *I Am* beautiful. *I Am* worthy. *I Am* qualified. *I Am* strong."

"What about you? What's your self-talk? What are you saying to yourself in the mirror?" asks Kenny. "Many of these women have children who are watching them and listening to them, and they pick up on all the things they say and do and replicate it."

Who do you believe you truly are? Kenny says, "I asked my wife recently, 'When do you feel the most confident?' She said, 'When I'm not thinking of myself.' When you're not thinking about yourself is when you truly know who you are because you're not worried about yourself." Now, you now have the opportunity to help others be better.

Many years ago, relates Kenny, Dan McCormick introduced him to Og Mandino's Scrolls. "I started reading them, and when I read, '*I Am* Nature's Greatest Miracle,' it made me think: '*I Am* more than just this person on this planet. God was specific about creating me with my talents and genius as much as he was clear about creating every fish in the sea, every plant, animal, person, and organism. He was that specific in creating *me*. I have gifts no one else has, and I can use those gifts in ways that help others.' That's the way a person or a plant grows and becomes Nature's greatest miracle. You and I were put on this planet for a purpose. Do you know what that is?"

Kenny's hope for his children when life hits them hard is that they'll be driving down the street and stop at a stop sign. And in that moment, an affirmation will jolt them and bring tears to their eyes. "In the Scriptures it says, 'Be still and know that *I Am*.' And when that happens, they'll immediately shift whatever they are going through. They'll know who they are. They'll know that we are Nature's greatest miracle, and we all are put on this earth for a purpose."

Notice that Kenny Brady's hope for his children has nothing to do with position or possessions and everything to do with knowing who they are—awakening who they are at every stop sign, to know the Great *I Am* and to shift from tears and fears to faith in future miracles.

HOW TO BECOME "CAPABLE"

WINNING IN THE MARGINS

The fact is: You don't need a fortune to have sufficient wealth and live well in health. Once you stop buying useless stuff, you become financially independent much faster. Best-selling author Richard Paul Evans calls it "winning in the margins."

Indeed, once we age beyond the accumulation phase, we want to downsize and simplify. We don't need all this stuff; in fact, we get rid of stuff we don't need or want anymore. As they say, "We can't take it with us when we die." (Have you ever seen a hearse with luggage racks?) You might sell or donate some of your possessions if they are just taking up space. After a while, you don't own your stuff—it owns you. So, you would happily trade having more stuff for having the capability and synergy that supplies sufficient health and wealth.

BECOME "CAPABLE" TODAY

THE POWER BEHIND THE AFFIRMATION

When you affirm, "*I Am* capable," you are saying to yourself: *I Am* qualified and capable, and I have the skills and abilities to succeed in anything I set my mind to. *I Am* confident in my abilities and trust that I can navigate any challenges that come my way.

I work hard to hone my skills and gain wisdom and a wealth of knowledge through my experiences. *I Am* proactive, resourceful, and innovative. *I Am* ready to take on any task that comes my way, knowing I have what it takes to succeed.

My confidence comes from a deep understanding of my strengths and weaknesses, and I use this self-awareness to my advantage. In areas where I need to improve, *I Am* proactive in seeking additional training, mentorship, or resources.

I Am a responsible and reliable team member who always seeks ways to improve team performance. I listen actively, communicate effectively, and collaborate seamlessly to promote a positive and supportive work environment.

I approach challenges with a growth-oriented mindset, knowing every obstacle is an opportunity for growth and learning. *I Am* a problem solver and quick thinker who can adapt to new situations with ease.

I Am creative and innovative, always seeking new ways to approach problems and tasks. *I Am* a strategic thinker who can see the big picture while also paying attention to the small details that are important for success.

I Am committed to achieving my goals and excelling in my roles. *I Am* passionate about what I do and strive to make a positive impact.

I also acknowledge my strengths and weaknesses, accepting that *I Am* not flawless and always seeking to learn and improve. I accept constructive criticism as an opportunity for self-reflection and growth.

Yes, *I Am* qualified and capable, with the skills, knowledge, and mindset to achieve great things. *I Am* always seeking new ways to grow, learn, and apply my unique strengths and abilities.

AFFIRMATION IN ACTION

As you affirm, *I Am* capable, reflect on your talents, skills, and capabilities and list them in your *I Am* Journal. Consider what might be the best and highest use of your capabilities. Also consider one capability you want to improve and create an action plan for strengthening it.

SUMMARY

- As we age, we can still shine the brightest by retraining and retaining capability.

- Synergy allows us to create new alternatives, options, and possibilities.
- When driving, say an affirmation at each stop sign.
- When you affirm, "*I Am* capable," you are saying to yourself: *I Am* qualified and capable. I have the skills and abilities to succeed in anything I set my mind to. *I Am* confident I can navigate any challenges that come my way.

— CHAPTER 10 —

I AM COMPASSIONATE

"The nature of humanity, its essence, is to feel another's pain as one's own, and to act to take that pain away. There is nobility in compassion, a beauty in empathy, a grace in forgiveness."

— John Connolly

DAY 6
I AM COMPASSIONATE **Loving, Accepting, Caring, Considerate, Charitable, Benevolent, Generous, Kind, Long-Suffering**

WELCOME TO FRIDAY: PAYDAY

Friday, in English, is named after Frigg or Freya, the Norse goddess of love. In Romance languages, it's named after Venus (*vendredi* in French), the ancient Roman goddess of love and beauty, counterpart to the Greek goddess Aphrodite. The planet Venus was named for the most beautiful of the ancient gods because it *shines the brightest* of the five planets that were known to ancient astronomers.

Even as we age, we can still shine the brightest, not only by using the best anti-aging products but also by retraining and retaining capability. Along with courage and confidence, we need character and compassion.

Inspiring leaders lead with compassion. Compassion goes beyond the notions of sympathy and empathy and calls upon the power of charity, which never fails.

WHAT DOES IT MEAN TO BE "COMPASSIONATE"?

The word *compassion* finds its roots in the Latin term *compati*, meaning "to suffer with." True compassion involves experiencing and understanding others' pain and struggles. This understanding drives us to extend kindness, support, and love to those in need.

The word *empathetic* originates from the Greek term "em-," meaning "in," and "pathos," meaning "feeling." We embrace empathy as the ability to enter into the feelings and experiences of others. Empathy is not merely understanding, but rather, actively engaging with the emotional landscape of another person, allowing me to provide comfort and aid with greater insight and sensitivity.

Em also means "to stand on," and *Pathy* means "someone's path." To stand on someone's path is to see through their eyes and gain a new perspective.

THE COMPASSION AFFIRMATION IN ACTION

JUDE: AN ADMONITION AND AFFIRMATION

Dan: Our fourteenth grandchild is named Jude, and so he came with his own admonition and affirmation (Jude 1:19-22):

> These be they who separate themselves, sensual, having not the Spirit. But ye, beloved, building up yourselves on your most holy faith, praying in the Holy Ghost, keep yourselves in the

> love of God, looking for the mercy of our Lord Jesus Christ unto eternal life. And of some have compassion, making a difference.

With Jude, I can attest: Those who lead and love with compassion do make a difference.

INVICTUS: EMPATHY ENACTED

Ken: Recently, Dan and I met a compassionate couple from South Africa who had only been in direct sales for five years, had already achieved Emerald status, and were projected to achieve Diamond level in another six months. The man was large, so I asked him if he had ever played rugby.

"Yes," he said, "I once played rugby."

I said, "You would make a big impact on anybody you meet" (as much for his compassion as his size).

We talked about the 2009 movie *Invictus*, about the 1995 South African rugby team, the Springboks, which was not expected to perform well in the Rugby World Cup hosted by South Africa and its president, Nelson Mandela. At the time, the home team struggled. President Mandela also faced enormous challenges in the post-Apartheid era, including rampant poverty and crime, along with racial divisions and tensions. He saw the rugby tournament as a chance to unite the country. Mandela affirmed his team's victory and shared with team captain François Pienaar the William Ernest Henley poem "Invictus," which had inspired him during his time in prison.

The poem ends with this affirmation:

> *I Am* the master of my fate: *I Am* the captain of my soul.

The inspired Springboks shocked the rugby world by winning the World Cup. Mandela and Pienaar met on the field after the game to celebrate the improbable victory.

As I reflected on our chance meeting with the South African couple, I recalled Marianne Williamson's quote that is often misattributed to Mandela:

> Our deepest fear is not that we are inadequate. Our deepest fear is that we are powerful beyond measure. It is our light, not our darkness that most frightens us. We ask ourselves, 'Who am I to be brilliant, gorgeous, talented, fabulous?' Actually, who are you not to be? You are a child of God. Your playing small does not serve the world. There is nothing enlightened about shrinking so that other people won't feel insecure around you. We are all meant to shine, as children do. We were born to make manifest the glory of God that is within us. It's not just in some of us; it's in everyone. And as we let our own light shine, we unconsciously give other people permission to do the same. As we are liberated from our own fear, our presence automatically liberates others.

CORRELATION WITH COVEY'S HABIT 5: SEEK FIRST TO UNDERSTAND, THEN TO BE UNDERSTOOD

We are more compassionate when we seek first to understand, to listen with empathy and respect. In our interactions, we often prescribe a solution before we diagnose the problem. We don't seek to understand first—we typically seek first to be understood. We listen with the intent to reply, not understand. When we listen autobiographically—with our own perspective as our frame of reference—we tend to respond in one of four ways: 1) Evaluate: agree or disagree with what is said; 2) Probe: Ask questions from our own frame of reference; 3) Advise: Give counsel based on our own experience; and 4) Interpret: Project motives and behavior based on our motives and behavior.

The second part of Habit 5 is to be understood—to have others deeply understand us and our perspective. This is also vital to achieving Win-Win solutions and outcomes.

SPOTLIGHT: XANDER CLARK

Xander Clark is a prime example of finding the right partner. He often affirms: "*I Am* Partnering with God."

Xander grew up in Mission Viejo, California, and attended Tesoro High School where he played on back-to-back CIF championship football teams and cherished the time he spent with friends and teammates. After he graduated from high school and seminary at age nineteen, he received a call to serve a church mission in Taiwan. Six weeks into his training, he experienced sharp pains in his stomach. The diagnosis shocked him: he had an umbilical hernia and needed to have it repaired immediately.

After the surgery, he started taking pain pills; and three weeks later, his wound became infected. He was put on antibiotics and told, "We can't send you to Taiwan; you'll serve in the Provo, Utah mission for six weeks and let it heal."

Within hours of meeting his new missionary companions, Xander passed out and was rushed to the hospital. His white blood cell count was four times what it was supposed to be!

His body had rejected the mesh they put in for hernia repair, and he underwent emergency surgery. Doctors removed the mesh, left the wound open to heal on its own, and sent him home for recovery.

Xander recalls: "I was devastated. I arrived at the Orange County airport with an open hole in my stomach and in pain. I came down the escalator and no one was waiting for me. No banners. No family or friends. I felt I had failed myself, my family, and my God. I affirmed: *I Am a failure!* When I went to church two days later, I had to answer questions from well-meaning members: 'Why are you home? When are you going back?' Rumors were going around; meanwhile I still had a hole in my stomach."

Daily, Xander had to get the dressing in his wound changed and repacked. Taking pain meds helped him deal with the pain and with his feelings of failure and inadequacy. By the time his wound healed, he was already on the path to opiate addiction.

Over the next five years, Xander cut himself off from family, friends, church, and God. "I hated who I had become and pushed everyone away from me," he said. "I still had a lot of resentment for what happened to me at the start of my mission."

One year later, his addiction to pain meds worsened, and he went headfirst into the sand while bodyboarding at Salt Creek Beach, bulging four discs in his neck.

This accident was a golden ticket to all the pain meds he ever wanted, but there was never enough. He went from doctor to doctor getting prescriptions to feed his $500-a day opiate addiction, and it controlled every aspect of his life. "When I looked in the mirror, I didn't recognize myself. I didn't want to live anymore. I landed myself on the DEA watch list for doctor shopping. I would run out of pills and be forced to get clean. Every time I would get off pills, I would commit to stay off. But within sixty days I couldn't bear the pain and would go back on pills. Finally, I got to this place where I became a shell of a person. All my friends had written me off. My family didn't want to be around me. I didn't want to be around myself. I wasn't who I used to be. I was by myself in my parents' house, using drugs, cooped up in the bedroom."

At that low point, Xander wanted to go to AA, but he did not want to talk about God. "I was still mad at God, and I felt that God was also angry at me. For four years, I avoided recovery programs because they talk about a Higher Power. AA is a faith-based sobriety program built on a power greater than yourself. When I first went to AA, I heard other people talking about God as a loving and forgiving Heavenly Father. I thought, maybe I need to reframe my view of God. Maybe he's not mad at me; maybe he doesn't resent me; maybe he still loves me."

Xander visited with his bishop, who told him, "Xander, I want you to go *into business with God. I want you to make God your business partner.*"

For some reason, that resonated with him. "I'm a serial entrepreneur, and I love business," said Xander. "I didn't want to give God total control, but I was willing to give him 51 percent control. As time went on, I realized the more control I gave God, the better off our business was. Today, my goal is to give him 100 percent, but I still get in the way, my pride, my ego, I'll take some back. It's a constant give and take."

Now, Xander affirms: *I Am* a partner with God. "At the end of the day, partnering with God was my best decision: I give him control, and all he asks for is 10 percent? What a deal!"

Sober since December 12, 2012, Xander runs the addiction recovery program in his area and sponsors several guys. "Recovery—along with family, business, and church—are the main pillars of my life. I was always a mover and a shaker in sales. I remember thinking, *When I get sober, I'll stop selling.* I thought selling was evil. While some sales tactics can be misleading, you can be an honest salesman, add a ton of value to people's lives, and have integrity."

When things were at their worst, recalls Xander, "I didn't feel qualified to be forgiven or worthy to have success. Through my addiction and my resentment toward God, I never lost my belief or faith. I felt like the Heavenly Father and the Savior loved everybody else, but I no longer qualified. I had lost self-love and self-confidence."

You, too, may feel you don't belong, you don't fit in, or you'll never measure up to high standards or the expectations of others. You may impose unrealistic expectations on yourself and think your worth is based on certain achievements.

When people come to AA, they will say, "*I Am* an addict. *I Am* programmed this way." *In The 7 Habits of Highly Effective People*, Stephen R. Covey says, "We are our own programmers." We hold the keys to the software to reprogram. We can rewire ourselves. It doesn't matter what your childhood was, you can change where you are and who you've been.

In his recovery, Xander affirms: "*I Am* rewiring the programming. Who *I Am* today is not the guy I was ten years ago. *I Am* happy, *I Am* joyous, *I Am* free. I've worked through a lot and gained so much knowledge and wisdom. In our recovery meetings, we have people as old as eighty-four who have changed their lives in ways they never thought they would or could. We deal with general addictions like drugs and alcohol, pornography and sex, food, codependency, gambling, even video games. When you identify as an addict, you confess you're powerless, meaning you can't control it. You say, 'I want to stop,' and you can't stop—your life becomes unmanageable."

In 2012, Xander's sister invited him to a church meeting where Andy Reid, the head coach of the Kansas City Chiefs, would be speaking. "I hadn't been inside a church for years, but I jumped at the chance to meet and hear Coach Reid. Two weeks after Coach Reid spoke at church, one of his sons overdosed and died on the same drugs I had been battling for years. This shook me because I knew this was the outcome I would face if I didn't get sober."

Xander started attending the church addiction recovery program and AA regularly; there he met people working to overcome hardships and addictions and grow closer to God.

A year and a half into sobriety, Xander went to school at BYU Hawaii where he met his wife, Courtney. "When Courtney and I bought our home in Mission Viejo, I was asked to run the recovery program. I'm in the trenches of spiritual warfare. I regularly attend AA meetings and serve others in recovery. I also go to jails, hospitals, and rehabs to share hope with those who are in the grips of addiction. I've also had to attend multiple funerals of those who died due to addiction. I've had multiple overdoses and should have died on more than one occasion. But I'm here, and I'm going to help those still struggling every day."

When Xander looks back, he recognizes the Lord's hand. "He never left me, although sometimes I felt alone. He sent angel after angel after angel to rescue me. Many people saw my potential when I was too lost to see it myself. I don't know why *I Am* so lucky and blessed.

"Your story won't be my story, but I promise you—hard times will come at some point, and you will be left with nothing to rely on except your faith. We all face temptations daily, and we all fall short. Having to repent doesn't make you weak. It makes you strong and allows you to feel the spirit. We can feel joy in spite of disappointments and setbacks along the way. We can be of good cheer; for Christ has overcome the world."

HOW TO BECOME "COMPASSIONATE"

FIND A COMPASSIONATE PARTNER

We consider the two most important decisions you can make in life to be: 1) find the right (compassionate) marriage partner; and 2) find the right (compassionate) business partner.

Again, you can rarely get to where you want to go alone—it takes a committed, covenant-based, and compassionate relationship. It's not good to be alone. Prosperity requires partnerships that work for both parties. Few people succeed in life without partners who share the same passion.

The worst thing about having the wrong work or wrong partner is that it saps your energy and ambition. What gets you through dark times is not to surrender your ambitions but to strengthen your relationships and partnerships. Do you have a compassionate partner and team you trust—ones that encourage you to be the best you can be?

What is the "full measure" of your creation? What is the optimal measure—your best and highest potential and promise? You will likely never achieve the full measure of your creation without finding compassionate partners.

BECOME "COMPASSIONATE" TODAY

THE POWER BEHIND THE COMPASSION AFFIRMATION

When you affirm, "*I Am* compassionate," you are saying to yourself: As I embody compassion and empathy, I strive to demonstrate their transformative power in my daily life. I approach every interaction with an open heart and an open mind, recognizing that we all carry unique burdens and experiences. I consciously choose to look past surface-level appearances, seeking to understand the deeper motivations and emotions.

To be compassionate and empathetic is an active practice. That means extending a helping hand in times of need. I offer comfort and support through acts of kindness, both big and small, always seeking to make a positive impact on those around me. By embodying empathy and compassion, I become an agent of healing and understanding, spreading warmth and love.

Moreover, my journey toward compassion and empathy is informed by continual self-reflection and growth. Developing and nurturing these qualities in myself is essential to developing them in others. I practice deep self-care and self-compassion, listening to my own needs and honoring them. By tending to my well-being, I cultivate the inner strength and resilience necessary to hold space for others with authenticity and presence.

I appreciate compassion and empathy's deep connection to unity and healing. I manifest these qualities in my personal relationships, and I advocate for social justice, standing up for the rights and well-being of marginalized communities. I actively work toward dismantling systems of oppression while embodying the interconnectedness of humanity and the power we hold to create a more compassionate and empathetic society.

I affirm: *I Am* compassionate and empathetic. I recognize that true compassion requires a willingness to bear the suffering of others. By practicing compassion and empathy, I foster healing within myself and contribute to a kinder and more interconnected world. Through these qualities I express my full potential and contribute to the betterment of society.

AFFIRMATION IN ACTION

When affirming *I Am* compassionate, think of a recent time when you showed compassion and when someone showed compassion to you. Reflect on how giving and receiving compassion makes you feel. Record these incidents and impressions in your I Am Journal. Also, note how you will show compassion this day or week to your loved ones, partners, or teammates. You might schedule a time for this compassionate service.

SUMMARY

- Inspiring leaders lead with compassion.
- Embrace empathy as the ability to enter into the feelings and experiences of others.
- We are more compassionate when we seek first to understand, to listen with empathy and respect.
- Partner with God. The more control you give God, the better things will be.
- Find compassionate partners who encourage you to be your best.

SECTION IV

WIN THE WEEK
And Your Life
(Fitness and Sustainability)

In this final section, we focus on an affirmation for winning each and every week.

AFFIRMATION 7: *I Am* a Finisher.

— CHAPTER 11 —

I AM A FINISHER

"There are better starters than me, but I'm a strong finisher."

— Usain Bolt

DAY 7
I AM A FINISHER **Fitness, Endurance, Energetic, Healthy, Athletic, Happy, Joyful, Diligent, Disciplined, Unstoppable, Force of Nature, Determined, Persistent, Resilient, Sustainable**

WELCOME TO SATURDAY

Saturday is named after Saturn, the god of agriculture in Roman mythology. In the context of Affirmation Week, we remind ourselves of the importance of organic growth, from seed and soil, from the ground up, in harmony with natural laws, principles, and processes.

So, Saturday is a day of maintenance—of turning the soil and changing the oil. For, as we all know, without maintenance, everything (including our bodies) tends to fall into disrepair. Saturday is also a day of washing and cleaning, running errands, doing service projects, shopping and exercising.

Saturday is also a day for some wholesome fun, entertainment, diversion, recreation, games, play, sport, contests, hobbies, music, singing, and dancing. We all need connection to other people and causes, societies and clubs, and friends and family. So, make a date, plan an event, and give yourself and your family and friends something to look forward to. Anticipation can keep you alive and well. A healthy social life sustains your life and keeps you young. Whole health is the aim, since health is such a big component of wealth; without health, there can be no sustainable wealth.

WHAT DOES IT MEAN TO BE "A FINISHER"?

This affirmation represents the execution of any creation and, hence, is the crescendo, the most important affirmation ever written for any project, business, or fitness goal. It is where the rubber meets the road. The highest values in life can be attributed to those things we finish.

Affirm: I finish what I start. Becoming a finisher is the culmination of the seven affirmations. We all want to finish the good projects, tasks, and relationships we start. Yet many people seem to think quitting is so easy. But plenty of mental anguish is associated with quitting. And it shreds our confidence for starting the next time after we just quit something else.

THE FINISHER AFFIRMATION IN ACTION

BRITISH CYCLING TEAM'S WINNING STRATEGY: WEEKLY 1 PERCENT IMPROVEMENTS

Little daily improvements can add up and make a big difference. For example, Dave Brailsford was hired in 2010 to be the coach for Team Sky, the Great Britain cycling team, and he was charged with winning the Tour de France. Great Britain had never had any cyclist win the Tour de France. He decided, "Okay, I'm going to set a goal that within five years, we'll have somebody from Great Britain win the Tour de France."

Brailsford didn't have to wait five years. He did it in three years when Bradley Wiggins rode across the finish line and won the Tour de France in 2012. The next year, teammate Chris Froome won it the second time for Great Britain. In between the two consecutive wins, they had the Olympics in 2012. Great Britain's Team Sky won 70 percent of the medals. That decade was the greatest ten years in cycling history for any country!

How did they do it? They put together a winning strategy. The coach said, "If we can focus on making 1 percent improvements, just 1 percent, if everybody can get 1 percent better consistently week after week, then we can do it." It wasn't just getting 1 percent faster on their times. They first looked at diet, at the nutrition that was going in. They looked at the seat on the bike and the weight of the bike, the aerodynamics of the bike, their helmets, and their training regimes. They looked at everything and asked, "How do we make this 1 percent better?" They started looking in other places. They started looking at the pillows the cyclists were sleeping on, and they started taking those pillows with them to every hotel. They started washing their hands regularly so they didn't get infections and didn't get sick, so they could train better and be further ahead. This was the depth that they went to in looking how they could improve just 1 percent every week.

See, that little 1 percent compounds over time, and it becomes powerful. When we are 1 percent better today, we don't notice it, do we? In the short run being 1 percent better or 1 percent worse isn't very noticeable. But these micro-improvements compound over time: you can get 1 percent better every week or you can get 1 percent better every day. With compounding, when we go out a year, two years, five years, we're talking a huge difference in the results that people have. It's not always just improving 1 percent to the upside. Sometimes eliminating mistakes we make on the downside can be as effective as making the improvements on the upside. We eliminate bad habits, negative thinking, some things we shouldn't be eating. Such little things can make a big impact long term by removing negatives, as well as improving the positives we hope to achieve.

Here's another way to think about it: A race is run, and a climb is done one step at a time. And often it's a long race, a marathon, not a sprint, and you can't sprint the whole marathon. It takes time; it's a process. When you think about climbing Mount Everest, consider what it takes. Most climbers have first climbed many other smaller mountains. When they go to Everest, they go to base camp and acclimate for a couple of weeks to get used to the altitude. Then they make some attempts up to the first base camp, and back and then up to the next base camp and back. They may do this over weeks before they decide to summit.

Every significant thing we do takes time, one step at a time. In fact, there is no real shortcut to success. Many people want to short circuit or figure out a better or different way.

Success results from having a few simple disciplines practiced every day. We just take these simple steps and repeat them every day over and over again. We try to get better at them while we're doing them. Sometimes there are definitely improvements we can make.

There is power in small wins and slow gains. Success doesn't have to be meteoric or the brightest star in the universe. In fact, it's almost better that it's not. We see many people come into our business. Some have rapid success, and they're not mature enough in the business to sustain it. Then they get discouraged because it doesn't always go that fast. They start to think, *What's wrong with me? What am I doing wrong now? It's not moving the way it used to move for me.* You may have fast success, or you may have success that comes later in your journey.

Don't get too excited about early success, and don't get too discouraged about not having much early success. If you're committed for the long term and continue doing these consistent things, eventually, you will have success!

This is why average speed yields above-average results. It's that compounding effect of learning those good, consistent habits. When you have a system in place, the system guides those daily repetitive actions that compound every day, that 1 percent improvement that leads to success. We're just looking for those little improvements over time. Daily affirmation and consistent action enable you to accomplish goals. Mastering habits is more important than achieving a certain outcome. You can program your subconscious mind with those goals by repeatedly reading them and putting them in your brain. It changes your thinking.

CORRELATION WITH COVEY'S HABIT 7: SHARPEN THE SAW

To continue to be effective, we renew ourselves physically, spiritually, mentally, and socially. These four dimensions of our nature must be exercised regularly in balanced ways.

Habit 7 is focused on taking time to ***sharpen the saw***. We enhance our greatest asset—ourselves. The aim of physical improvement is to exercise our body in a way that will enhance our capacity to work, adapt, and enjoy. We eat well, get sufficient rest and relaxation, and exercise regularly. Renewing our spiritual self enables us to provide leadership to our life and reinforces our commitment to our value system. We practice daily meditation, communicate with nature, read great literature, or listen to music. By renewing our mental health, we expand our minds. By renewing ourselves socially, we develop meaningful relationships. We seek to understand other people, make contributions to meaningful projects, and maintain an abundance mentality. We serve others and make deposits of love and trust in their emotional bank accounts.

Changing our perspective changes our behavior, and our behaviors produce our outcomes, which shape our lives. In order to improve behaviors, we first examine and shift our paradigms, the lenses through which we see the world, interpret our situations and surroundings, and influence our behavior. Enduring success rests on the character ethic (integrity, humility, fidelity, courage, temperance, justice, patience, industry, simplicity, modesty, and the Golden Rule)—as opposed to the personality ethic (personality, public image, public relations, attitudes, and behaviors).

SPOTLIGHT: NATHAN RICKS

As I, Dan, think of being a finisher, I think of my close friend Nathan Ricks, who tragically died in a plane crash in 2023. He was a finisher, and he taught me much about finishing both by precept and by example. Here is a digest of his classic *Be a Finisher* speech:

What does it mean to be a finisher? Finishers are people like Mahatma Gandhi and Nelson Mandela—people who faced difficult tasks, things that people told them were impossible. Yet they stuck with it, continued to press forward, and finished strong.

It's easy to start something, but it's much harder to finish. It's easy to start a project. We find something that looks cool and get all excited about it. Then in a month or two, we start to lose the energy and excitement. Why? Because it's easy to start and hard to finish. It's not easy to do the mundane tasks that it takes to do it over and over again and to take it to the end.

I'm sure that Mother Teresa, Gandhi, and Mandela had many days that weren't fun, many days when they were just trying to press forward to keep the commitment. That day-to-day consistency separates successful people from those people who don't accomplish their goals.

It's easy to dismiss the value of making slightly better decisions daily. Sticking with the fundamentals is not impressive. Getting 1 percent better won't make the headlines. So many times we get excited about something, and we view success as doing something earth-shattering that gets front-page headlines, but that rarely happens, even with people who are finishers.

The final result doesn't happen in a day, week, or month. In many cases, it happens over a lifetime! It depends on what you want, right? It depends on your objective and what you're trying to accomplish. But whatever it is, there will be tough tasks and people we have to deal with.

HOW TO BECOME "A FINISHER"

SET MAGIC GOALS

At the University of Chicago, two psychology professors did some research that was published in *Harvard Business Review*. It talks about "to go" versus "to date." What does that mean? When we look at goals that we write down, objectives we want to accomplish, there's a journey involved in getting from where we start to accomplish the goal. Most people look at what they've done so far. That's called to date. They look at what they've accomplished to date. They look back and say, "Look at how far I've come. That's really great!"

That tends to make you satisfied. It doesn't leave you as motivated to go out and accomplish the rest of the journey and get to your goal. They suggest you should look at what's left to go versus what you've done to date. Look forward, look at the landscape you still have to travel over, and realize where you've got to go. Then decide that is what you're going to do and keep focused on the goal.

When you note how far you've come in achieving your goal and you look forward to how far you still have to go, your mind recognizes the gap and starts to get more focused. You become more earnest in what you're trying to accomplish. You have more motivation. You're more driven and focused.

Setting a goal is like magic. If you write down your goal, read and affirm it every day, and take action every day, you can accomplish almost anything. You start to see things differently. You start to believe you can achieve things you never thought were possible for yourself. It's all about changing your mind, the way you think, allowing yourself to believe it's possible. You need to give yourself permission to be as successful as you can be. Are you willing to give yourself permission? You have to love yourself enough. To know that when you do that, it's not just going to be good for you; it's going to be good for many other people.

People always want me to tell them the secret. The secret is there are no secrets. That's the secret! What we have to do is simply do more of what works, including what is boring and mundane. These are simple steps. We just need to stay focused and repeat them. We just need to do more of what already works! We know what works for us. When people tell me, "I've got this idea," I say, "No, I've seen this movie a million times. I don't want to see the movie anymore. Just do it this way. Just follow these steps. Make your first million our way. After that, you can make the second and third million any way you want."

CONSISTENT IMPROVEMENT

Being consistent daily enables us to eat the elephant—that great big goal. We eat the elephant one bite at a time or one day at a time, one step at a time every day.

That's why we keep a journal—to keep track of what we do—because the numbers don't lie. If we tell a story to ourselves enough, we believe our own lie. We think we're really working really hard. What we're working hard doing is thinking about our work instead of doing our work. When it comes to finishing, rule number one is don't start so many things. The biggest wastes of time in our lives are all of the projects we start and never finish. We never take them to the finish line. All that effort goes wasted because we never take it to the finish line. This is the danger of trying to take on too many things, trying to start too many things.

Most people cannot be consistent. They can't discipline themselves to stick to the task. I like the anonymous poem:

Stick to your task 'til it sticks to you;
Beginners are many, but enders are few.
Honor, power, place and praise
Will come, in time, to the one who stays.

Stick to your task 'til it sticks to you;
Bend at it, sweat at it, smile at it, too.
For out of the bend and the sweat and the smile
Will come life's victories, after awhile.

Associate with people who have similar goals and move forward together. You will become the average of your five closest friends—the five people you spend the most time with. You need to consider who those people are in your life now. You need to associate with people who are positive, who are moving forward, who are consistent in what they do, and who can inspire you to do these same things yourself.

Experiences with positive people and positive energy will change the way you think. The will change your vision of how big you see the business for yourself. When you listen to other people with whom you can identify, who are like you, it gives you license to think you can do the same thing.

Nothing big will happen overnight. It takes time and a path, process, or system. Since many things will impact your life, you have to work hard. You won't accomplish anything great with casual efforts. Casual efforts result in casualties. So, choose to be a finisher. Choose to show up every day until the job is done. Don't look back at how far you've come. Focus on what's still ahead, what's still in front of you to go there. That'll create that gap in your mind. It'll keep you focused. It'll keep you moving forward so you can achieve rich rewards long term.

THE LIFE-CHANGING BENEFITS OF AFFIRMING "I AM A FINISHER"

HEALTH-WEALTH CONNECTION

We all want the story line of our life to lead naturally from Roots to Fruits.

So, today, Saturday, we all want to enjoy the fruit and produce of our faith and work, our toil in soil. The condition of the soil is the focus of Christ's *Parable of the Sower:*

> Behold, a sower went forth to sow; And when he sowed, some seeds fell by the way side, and the fowls came and devoured them up: Some fell upon stony places, where they had not much earth: and forthwith they sprung up, because they had no deepness of earth: And when the sun was up, they were scorched; and because they had no root, they withered away. And some fell among thorns; and the thorns sprung up and choked them: But other fell into good ground, and brought forth fruit, some a hundredfold, some sixtyfold, some thirty-fold. Who hath ears to hear, let him hear.

What we like about this parable is the payoff potential on the bottom line: thirty times, sixty times, or even one hundred times. This is not an incremental difference—it's an exponential difference.

You plant seeds of wealth in the soil of your mind when you make positive affirmations and then pray for their productivity night and day.

BECOME A "FINISHER" TODAY

THE POWER BEHIND THE AFFIRMATION

When you affirm, "*I Am* a Finisher," you are saying to yourself, "I have the tenacity, perseverance, and determination to see things through to completion. Whether it's a task at work, a personal project, or a lifelong dream, I have what it takes to keep going until the end."

I face challenges that test my resolve, but I have faith in my abilities and my commitments. I know that every step I take, no matter how small, brings me closer to my ultimate goal. And if I stumble or falter, I pick myself up and keep moving forward.

I do not let setbacks, roadblocks, or obstacles stop me. Instead, I see and use them as opportunities to learn, grow, and become stronger. I embrace challenges because they make me more determined to succeed.

Whether I'm working alone or as part of a team, I bring my best effort to every task. *I Am* reliable, innovative, and resourceful—always finding ways to get the job done efficiently and effectively. And when others need help or support, *I Am* there to offer a helping hand and empower them to succeed.

Every day, I remind myself that success is not just about reaching the finish line but about the journey along the way. I strive to enjoy every moment, appreciating small accomplishments that keep me moving forward.

I acknowledge my strengths and weaknesses, accepting that I have flaws and always seeking to learn and improve. I accept constructive criticism as an opportunity for self-reflection and growth.

As a finisher, *I Am* disciplined and organized, keeping track of my progress and setting realistic goals. I plan ahead and stay focused on the task at hand, even when distractions crop up, knowing that the more I stay on course, the faster I will reach my destination. *I Am* capable of so much more than I sometimes allow myself to believe. I look back on my accomplishments and feel proud of what I've achieved, knowing I have the strength and determination to do even more.

SHOW COMMITMENT: FINISH SOMETHING!

We encourage you to finish something, anything, today. Stop researching, planning, and preparing, and just do the work. You don't need to set the world on fire with your first try. You just need to prove to yourself that you have what it takes to produce and finish something. No artists, athletes, entrepreneurs, or scientists became great by half-finishing their work. So, stop debating what you should make and create and finish something. Let the seven *I Am* affirmations guide you. Retire to your bed early and arise early: Win the morning, win the day, win the week, and win your life. Follow your Savior, Jesus Christ, who "in the morning, rising up great while before the day, went out and departed into a solitary place and there prayed" (Mark 1:35).

Reflect on what Johann Wolfgang von Goethe wrote two centuries ago:

> Until one is committed, there is hesitancy, the chance to draw back, always ineffectiveness. Concerning all acts of initiative, there is one elementary truth, the ignorance of which kills countless ideas and splendid plans: that the moment one definitely commits oneself, then Providence moves too. All sorts of things occur to help one that would never otherwise have occurred. A whole stream of events issues from the decision, rising in one's favor: all manner of unforeseen incidents and meetings and material assistance, which no man could have dreamed would have come his way. Whatever you can do, or dream you can, *begin it (and finish it).* Boldness has genius, power, and magic in it!

AFFIRMATION IN ACTION

Each time you affirm *I Am a Finisher*, envision yourself finishing well a current project or perhaps a race, test, trial, task, or goal. Imagine how great you will feel or think of receiving some recognition or reward, more money or less worry. Think of one great finisher to emulate. In your *I Am* Journal, write about times in your life when you finish something worthwhile.

SUMMARY

- Becoming a finisher is the culmination of the seven affirmations.
- Strive for weekly 1 percent improvement.
- If you write down your goal, read and affirm it every day, and take action every day, you can accomplish almost anything.

- There is no secret. Just do more of what works, including the boring and mundane.

I invite you to become a finisher. I invite you to be a co-creator of this book by sharing your unique ideas, stories, and thoughts in your journal as an addition to this book.

— CHAPTER 12 —

WEEKLY RENEWAL

Affirmation Week Renews

Affirmation Week never ends—it only begins again on Sunday with the renewing of your vision, mission, promises, covenants, and affirmations—the pattern for creating and sustaining Whole Health and Wealth. On Sunday, you are open to new promptings and opportunities. While the *pattern* remains the same, the *particulars* change. Some bedrock principles and priorities and partners remain constant, but all else can change as needed to meet the demands of the new week. Throughout the week as you create and repeat your affirmations, keep in mind:

- Your affirmations must reflect your core personal values. Why repeat something arbitrary to yourself if it doesn't align with your sense of what you believe to be good, moral, and worthwhile?
- Writing your affirmations in a journal and practicing them in the mirror makes them even more powerful and effective. If you want to carry them with you during your day, make your own positive affirmation cards and have them in your wallet, purse, or pocket.
- Repeating your affirmations frequently encourages positive feelings, thoughts, and attitudes—and happy thoughts help create a healthy mind and body. While practicing affirma-

tions, take deep, slow breaths. As you become more attuned to the flow of your breath, focus on the affirmation you've created for yourself; each time you practice, it will feel more natural.

"If you want to change the way you feel about yourself, first you have to change the way you think about yourself."

— Gavin Bird

"Take positive care of your mind, and it will take positive care of your life."

— Edmond Mbiaka

"You've been criticizing yourself for years. Try approving of yourself and see what happens."

— Louise Hay

YOUR ONE-WEEK PATTERN

Your month, your year, your life will likely follow your *weekly pattern*. So, put your life into a wealth pattern—simply by living one whole week. You might affirm: Week after week, *I Am* being healed and becoming healthy and wealthy—in every way.

When you sense that you will be better off if you pursue a certain path, you will discipline yourself to get there. You access such energy through spiritual connection—and if you fail to act on your inspiration, you will lose your ability to receive it.

You are free to make your own choices, and your choices determine your destiny.

Your quantity of life (longevity) may be the result of chance (good genes), choice, or a combination of the two. However, your quality of life is affected by many factors, and it is more in your control than you imagine, even though you may be disabled or debilitated in some way. In truth, we are all handicapped in some way—we are all "differently-abled."

What might be the Full Measure of your life? How might you live a Full Life in order to fill the full measure or purpose of your creation? You affirm your worth, wealth, and health one affirmation, one morning, one day, and one week at a time—following a pattern that starts a virtuous, not a vicious cycle. You learn to win the morning, win the day, and win your life, week after week, positive affirmation after positive and powerful affirmation... such as this one:

AFFIRMATION: *I Am* Walking
Paralyzed Man Walks Again!

You may have heard about the Dutch man who was paralyzed in a cycling accident in 2011 and could not move his legs for twelve years. Then in 2023, he was able to walk once again after having electronic brain-spine implants and using his mind to think, *I am walking*, and to see himself walking.

Today, Gert-Jan Oskam is able to stand, walk, climb stairs, and traverse complex terrains again—just by thinking it, visualizing it, and affirming it.

He even has some control over his legs when the device is off. "My wish was to walk again, and I believed it was possible," Oskam said. He can now walk 100 meters.

The implant surgery was led by Swiss researcher and neurosurgeon, Professor Jocelyne Bloch, who said it may take a few years before the technology is widely available.

The team of researchers from Lausanne University has developed an algorithm that interprets the brain signals into instructions to move legs and other foot muscles.

Gert-Jan Oskam said that learning to walk once again was mesmerizing because he felt like a toddler learning to walk. This remarkable development is encouraging and could help millions of paralyzed individuals around the world.

Ken: In a sense, all of us are paralyzed to some degree. We have all had our share of accidents, illnesses, mistakes, setbacks, and failures—along with some sins, compulsions, or addictions—that may leave us paralyzed with tears and fears. We may wonder if we will ever be able to walk, talk, golf, or cycle again. Could it be that some smart electronic implant—programmed with some algorithm that interprets our brain's signals into instructions to stand, move, walk, talk, or climb—might help us perform again? I don't know, but I do know this: Our minds have an amazing power over matter and the matters of our life. And what often triggers this power is our faith, our positivity—"just thinking it," visualizing it, and affirming it as if it has already happened. I believe Gert-Jan Oskam is walking today, in part, because he tapped into the power of affirmation and visualization to overcome paralysis. All of us can do the same—and walk those 100 meters or 100 miles with smiles—by the power of daily affirmation and visualization (applied faith).

After winning his twenty-third tennis grand slam title in Paris, Serbia's Novak Djokovic said, "I've experienced many things on and off the court, been through many trials and tribulations. I want to leave you with a message of inspiration. Since I was seven years old, I was dreaming that I would win Wimbledon and become the number one tennis player in the world. I felt that I had the power to create my own destiny (through affirmation and visualization, positivity and energy), and I believed it with every cell in my body. If you want a better future, take the means in your hands and create it." He then went on to win his twenty-fourth grand slam title in New York.

HOW WILL YOU MEASURE YOUR LIFE?

When measuring success in life, Clayton Christensen, a Harvard Professor of Business Administration and our friend, advised the graduates of the university to "choose the right yardstick." He said: "This past year I was diagnosed with cancer and faced the possibility that my life would end sooner than I'd planned. This experience has given me important insight into my life. I have a clear idea of how my ideas have generated enormous revenue for companies; I know I've had a substantial impact. But as I've confronted this disease, I see how unimportant that impact is to me now. I've concluded that the metric by which God will assess my life isn't dollars but the individual people whose lives I've touched. I think that's the way it will work for us all. Don't worry about the level of individual prominence you have achieved; worry about the individuals you have helped become better people. Think about the metric by which your life will be judged and make a resolution to live every day so that in the end, your life will be judged a success."

WE HAVE POWER TO BE THE MIRACLE!

In the movie *Bruce Almighty*, Bruce loses his girlfriend Grace (by being an egoist), and God asks him: "Do you want her back?"

A reformed Bruce answers: "No. I want her to be happy, no matter what that means. I want her to find someone who will treat her with all the love she deserved from me. I want her to meet someone who will see her always as I do now, through Your eyes."

God affirms: "Now *that's* a prayer!"

And God explains: "Parting your soup is not a miracle, Bruce. It's a magic trick. A single mom who's working two jobs and still finds time to take her kid to soccer practice, that's a miracle. A teenager who says 'no' to drugs and 'yes' to an education, that's a miracle. People want me to do everything for them. But what they don't realize is *they* have the power. You want to see a miracle, son? Be the miracle."

So, please affirm: **"*I Am* the miracle...of my morning, day, week, and life!"**

And realize: We (you and I) have the power to be the miracle!

A FINAL NOTE

Go All In for Big Wins

AFFIRM:

"I Am a Magnet for Miracles!"

When we first discussed this book, we were thrilled to take a critical step ahead and compose the most genuine and authentic book ever written as to how to live any affirmation you think, say, or put on paper. We wanted to create a reliable affirmation guide to help all of us to be ***all in*** as entrepreneur Naval Ravikant is quoted as saying in James Clear's brilliant book *Atomic Habits*.

You, too, need to be "all in." If you are not *all in*, you'll likely settle for a *small win*.

Now, small wins are fine when we are first starting a new venture or habit. We need small wins—making more conservative goals and having incremental successes—to gain experience and build the confidence necessary to go for more challenging *stretch* or *moonshot* goals that involve more risk and may seem impossible to achieve with current capabilities or resources. We are more inclined to go for big wins when we have experienced recent success.

So, the question becomes: How can we employ affirmations to have more big wins?

SENSORY STACKING

At the start of the book, we wrote how the ***number 7*** is heavenly, and here we conclude the book with ***7 levels*** of affirmation and habit stacking that cements and concludes the process.

Dan: I recently experienced a breakthrough in affirmations. I call it ***Sensory Stacking***, a technique that explodes the power of affirmations by leveraging our inherent five senses—vision, hearing, taste, smell, and touch—and our "sixth sense" of mental perception and "seventh sense" of social connection. Hence, it ignites the power of ***7 senses***.

- ***Think it to attract it.*** Mental perception and autosuggestion follow the Law of Attraction.
- ***Say it to hear it.*** When you voice it, you hear it. The resonance of your voice creates a feedback loop that reinforces the positivity of your affirmations and imprints them into your subconscious mind.
- ***Write it to see it.*** When you see or envision your written affirmations written, it reinforces their importance and helps you visualize your desired outcomes.
- ***Feel it to touch it.*** Engaging your sense of touch adds a powerful tactile dimension to your affirmations, making them more visceral and memorable.
- ***Taste it to savor it.*** When you "taste" healing or taste abundance, you nourish your body with healthy choices and align your physical well-being with your abundance mindset.
- ***Smell it to incent it.*** When you smell your affirmation, you immerse yourself in uplifting scents, stimulate your olfactory senses, enhance your mood, and incent your action.

- ***Share it to sustain it.*** As you share your affirmations, you connect socially with others, spread the positive energy, sustain your forward momentum, and enhance your influence.

Sensory stacking builds on extensive research with the visual, auditory, and kinesthetic (VAK) learning style and model, which originated in the 1910s with the psychology of word recall and mental imagery and was developed further by educational psychologists in the 1920s, and again in the 1970s, for use in education and training to enhance learning experiences.

Visual (See It): Visualizing affirmations activates the creative centers of your brain, making your goals and desires more tangible. So, visualize your affirmations and write them down to create a tangible connection to them.

Auditory (Hear It): Speaking affirmations aloud harnesses the power of sound vibrations to manifest your intentions. You literally speak your affirmations into existence.

Kinesthetic (Feel It): When you physically interact with your affirmations by tracing them with your fingers or holding symbolic objects, you create a kinesthetic anchor that strengthens your emotional connection to your goals.

By incorporating visual, auditory, and kinesthetic elements into your affirmations, you create an immersive experience that resonates with you on multiple levels. Each sense serves as a gateway to deeper self-awareness and transformation, allowing you to tap into your innate potential, nurture healing, and cultivate abundance.

HABIT STACKING

Sensory Stacking also builds on the proven process of ***Habit Stacking***. We all know from experience that changing an old habit or creating a new habit is hard because we are wired for what we're already used to, already good at, or already familiar with.

Habit stacking involves *stacking* new behaviors onto current behaviors to access the strong synaptic connections in our brains, notes health and wellness expert Maggie Seaver. "These connections are strongest for behaviors we already practice and weakest for those we don't. When we identify a daily habit we already engage in and add a new habit before or after it, we capitalize on existing connections in our brain. The current habit serves as a cue to engage in the new habit; hence, the new habit feels like something we already do."

EXPERIMENT UPON OUR WORDS

If you have lingering doubts about the power of positivity and positive affirmations, we invite you to replicate two experiments, as conducted and reported by Hilary Weeks in YouTube video:

> ***Experiment 1: Clicking Negative and Positive Thoughts.***
>
> I once heard an inspirational speaker say that on average, we think some 300 negative thoughts a day. Wanting to know if that was accurate, I ordered a wrist clicker and counted my negative thoughts for one week. During the week, I clicked over 100 negative thoughts every day! By the end of the week, I felt depressed and wondered: Could counting my negative thoughts give them power to change my mood?
>
> That moment, I decided to change the experiment. I decided to click my positive or uplifting thoughts. On Day 1, I clicked 321 positive thoughts! And on Day 4, I was shocked when I saw the tally: 1,262! And during that week, my spirit seemed to soar.

I learned from my own experience that ***there is power in what we think***. Our thoughts affect our moods, behaviors, and choices. Positivity has become more natural for me now. And I can attest: Our thoughts, more than anything else, determine what we accomplish in life.

Experiment 2: Talking Naughty and Nice to Rice.

I once heard of an experiment originally conducted by Dr. Masaru Emoto, a renowned Japanese author who wanted to show the power of positive thoughts and words. I was intrigued and decided to replicate it.

This experiment involves two jars of cooked rice. One is labeled LOVE, the other HATE. The rice in the LOVE jar is showered with positive words; the rice in the HATE jar is showered with negative words or phrases. What happens? The rice in the LOVE jar stays fresh while the rice in the HATE jar rots faster. Think of it: ***Words alone did that!*** Unkind words repeated over and over.

Dan: When I saw Hilary Weeks' YouTube video, I decided to replicate the experiment, except I added an IGNORE jar. My results: The rice in the LOVE jar remained the same while the rice in the HATE jar started turning brown. And the rice in the IGNORE jar became downright nasty. Wow! It made me wonder, *What aspect of my life is being ignored?*

Our thoughts and emotions have a direct and powerful impact on our lives: our health, relationships, happiness, well-being, and self-esteem. Positive thoughts and emotions attract positive outcomes, while negative thoughts and emotions attract negative outcomes. By becoming aware of our thoughts and emotions, we can begin to change our patterns of thinking, and by making positive affirmations, we can generate more positive outcomes.

AFFIRM: I AM WORTHY

Why is it so important to affirm ***I Am Worthy***, even if you are infirm in some way, even if you have poor health, little wealth, low salary, low self-worth, low self-image, high sin, even if you feel unworthy or even worthless at the time?

Answer: You may need first to affirm your worth or worthiness before you can attain it. Affirmation leads to actualization. Belief leads to behavior. Positivity leads to proactivity. Of course, as important as it is to affirm worthiness, it's even more important to ***be worthy, whole and integral, to have integrity. It's far more important to be virtuous than to affirm virtue.***

You can say ***I am worthy***, but do you mean it? Do you feel it to be true? Do you feel worthy of your spouse, family, home, possessions, health, wealth? Do you feel worthy to be in the best places with the best company, among the noblest people?

AFFIRMATION STACKING

The affirmation I am worthy is the keystone of the 7 Affirmations:

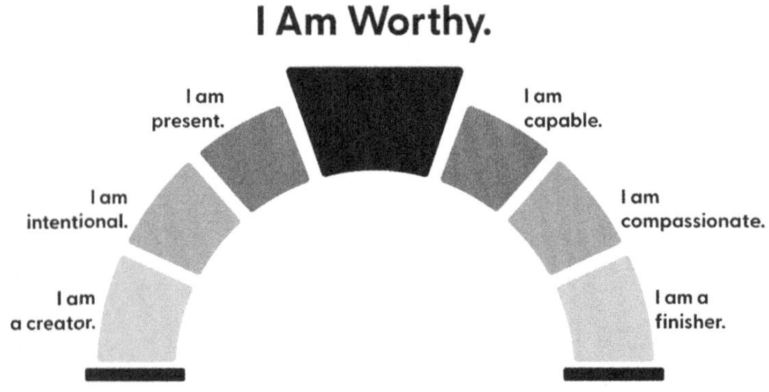

Literally, the ***keystone*** is the wedge-shaped piece at the crown of an arch that locks the other pieces in place. Metaphorically, the

keystone is the most important part of a plan or idea on which everything else depends. Like a keystone, the affirmation ***I am worthy*** keeps the other affirmations in place. Without this keystone, your personal ***Arc de Triomphe*** would collapse.

Many people forfeit health and wealth because they don't feel worthy due to low self-worth. If you sense a gap between the affirmation of your worth or your worthiness and your assessment of your actual current condition, consider what you might do to feel more worthy.

Why? Again, if you don't feel worthy of your win, you won't seek and attain win-win outcomes. So, rather than insist on *win-win or no deal*, you might seek to please and appease and settle for *lose-win* (I lose, you win) or *lose-lose* (We both lose).

Awakening expands your self-awareness and your feelings of self-worth, often leading to lifestyle changes, new habits, new interests, new relationships, new careers, and new sources of income. And your greatest awakening comes when you become aware of your infinite worth—and you feel worthy. You realize, as Anthon St. Maarten said: "You are a Divine Being, an all-powerful Creator. You are a Deity in jeans and a t-shirt, and within you dwells the infinite wisdom of the ages and the sacred creative force of All that is, will be and ever was."

"Awakening Who I Am" Movement Gains Momentum

You are now armed with ideas and tools for a lifetime of contributions. After reading an earlier draft of this book, friends, coworkers, and strangers started sharing within days the ***miracles*** they were seeing. People from all over the world are now affirming, *I am a magnet for miracles* simply because we asked them to write it, say it, and believe it.

Yes, the Awakening Who I Am movement is gaining momentum as thousands of people worldwide are clarifying what they want in their lives, stacking their affirmations, and using all of their senses to magnify who they are to achieve their small wins and their stretch goals.

The impact is overwhelming. So much so we revisited the amazing spotlight stories in the book to see if these people could relate to being magnets for miracles. Not only could they relate, but each of them could reveal additional miracles as they take a few minutes every day to make their affirmations on 7 levels.

We promise you: If you will invest 18 minutes a day and approximately 1 percent of your time—or what many people call *the rule of 100*—you will experience what Kim Cameron calls the ***heliotropic effect***—the tendency to move toward positive energy, to attract love and light into your life to illuminate your mindset and heart-set. You will feel worthy of your wins. As you become the book, you will see that it's all happening; it's all being created. And you will likely double or triple your income within one year.

Ralph Waldo Emerson wrote: "The mind, once stretched by a new idea, never returns to its original dimensions." And we affirm: Your heart and soul, once stretched by the ideas in this book, will never return to their original dimensions.

Ken Shelton

AFTERWORD

By Benjamin Hardy, PhD

AFFIRM YOUR FUTURE

Take Ownership of Your Future Self

As a rule, we tend to place extreme emphasis on our present selves. We tend to cling to our current identities and speak to ourselves and to others in incredibly definitive terms about who we are now: "*I Am* an introvert" or "*I Am* not good with people," etc. Those labels leave little wiggle room for change and growth—for becoming our future selves.

In this book, Dan McCormick and Ken Shelton remind us that our affirmations today create our Future Self. Our personality, skills, likes, and dislikes change over time—and that change is within our control. One thing we can do to become the version of ourselves we most want to be is to start affirming our future selves, believing the person we are today is not the person we will always be. You and I can be our Future Self now!

To make quality decisions, you need to know where those decisions will take you. Decisions and actions are best when reverse-engineered from a desired outcome. So, start with what you want and work backward. Think and act from your goal, rather than toward your goal. Your brain is like a "prediction machine," guiding your behavior toward your expected future.

The clearer you are on where you want to go, the less distracted you are by endless options. When you're disconnected from your Future Self, you get caught up in urgent goals that often result in poor present behavior. When you are disconnected from your Future Self, you opt for near immediate goals or dopamine hits. The more connected you are to your Future Self, the better you live in the present.

As Stephen R. Covey said, "Mental creation precedes physical creation." Anyone who creates something substantial does so by seeing it in their mind first, affirming it, and working toward the image. As they take steps forward, their vision clarifies, expands, and evolves.

Once you are clear and committed, everything filters through your goal or your selective attention. You see what you're looking for and what you care most about. What you focus on expands. Not only do you see what you're looking for, but you also act toward what you most want and have decided and affirmed will be yours.

FAITH MAKES THE FUTURE FLOW

The Bible says, "Faith is the substance of things hoped for, the evidence of things not seen." Whoever you are being now is the evidence of your Future Self. Your level of faith in and commitment toward your Future Self is evidenced by everything you do, and by every thought you think (your affirmations and self-talk).

Faith is a principle of action and power. By faith, you can make millions of dollars and heal impossible maladies. To exercise such faith, you need to fashion a vision of what you want. Know that whatever you want is already yours. Act as though everything you want can and will be yours. We fashion the future we envision for ourselves. We are driven by our views of the future. What future are you currently committed to? What if you chose something else? What if you committed to what you truly want?

When you commit 100 percent to what you want and know the end result is already yours, you will see evidence of the future you're creating. You'll stop associating pain with the work and changes required for your goals. Instead, you'll associate pain with not making progress toward your dreams. You'll associate pain with the short-term dopamine hits that were once your escape. You'll be far more courageous. You'll develop mentorships and collaborations with like-minded people. Your mindset, beliefs, and mental models will change, and you'll see the world far differently from how your former self saw it.

Also, your results will improve. You can know what you're committed to by your results. We are all committed. We are all producing results. The result is proof of a commitment. Your behavior will change because your identity has changed. Your identity is what you're most committed to. Your identity is based on the vision you have for yourself. When you change your committed vision, your identity immediately changes, which, in turn, immediately changes the flow of your thoughts and behaviors.

Yes, it requires courage to fully embrace your Future Self. Yes, it sometimes takes more time than you anticipated. Yes, there will be obstacles. But if you're committed, everything you face along the way will only better prepare you for what you truly want. Everything that comes at you will strengthen your resolve. You'll turn any experience to your gain, moving you further and evolving you beyond what you could initially imagine. When you're 100 percent committed and have faith, you will find the way.

There is always a way. As Ralph Waldo Emerson said, "When you make a decision, the universe conspires to make it happen."

NOW, CREATE YOUR FUTURE SELF

We are not the byproducts of our past. It's not the past that drives us, but rather, it is the future that pulls us. We have the unique ability to imagine countless future scenarios for ourselves. We can imagine staying in our current job, leaving the country, starting a business, or millions of other prospects. Despite having countless future potentials, our present is ultimately pulled forward by the future we're most committed to.

Your "default future" is what you are committed to—not what you hope will happen. It's what you've already decided and fully expect will happen. You have a future ahead of you that you've already fully bought into. And that future is the cause of everything you're doing now.

Every human action is toward an end, goal, or outcome. So, you can know what you're committed to by observing your behavior since your behavior reflects your commitment. To change your behavior, you need to shift the future that is pulling you forward. If you're not connected to a long-term vision, how could you possibly know what to do with your time? If you don't know where you're trying to go, how can you know where to direct your attention?

You are being pulled forward by the future you are most committed to. Your default future is what you expect to happen, even if it's not what you want to happen. Your behavior reflects the future you are most committed to. If you are not connected to your longer-term future self, you tend to make stupid and short-sighted decisions in the present.

If you want to make better decisions, connect with your Future Self. Recognize your Future Self is a different person than you are. Your Future Self sees the world differently than you do. They have different goals than you do. They have different experience, knowledge, and priorities. Hence, to develop a connection with your Future Self, you have empathy for them.

To make your Future Self more vivid, think about where you want to be in the near future, the next three to five years. What does your own "next level" look like? Define your three priorities, and then remove everything that conflicts or distracts from them.

In my and Dan Sullivan's book *10x Is Easier than 2x*, we note that while aiming for ten times the growth rather than two times the growth would seemingly require much more work, it's actually easier because it requires real change and transformation, not just doing more of what you're doing now. It's just not possible to work ten times harder and ten times longer to achieve ten times the growth.

So, achieving a ten times growth goal—exponential growth in your life and business—is actually easier than achieving a two times goal. To make ten times possible, you must focus on expanding what Sullivan defines as your four most important freedoms—time, money, relationship, and purpose. As your time becomes ten times more valuable, you increasingly multiply the money you earn both in terms of amount and profitable satisfaction.

As money becomes a tool you can increasingly access with greater ease, you will engage with a growing number of other freedom-motivated individuals. As life fills up with ten times more unique and collaborative relationships, you will realize your most powerful purposes in all areas become ten times more lasting and positive for everyone involved. You will be impressed by what your life has become and by the meaning and impact you're having.

As Dan McCormick and Ken Shelton advise us: Start thinking and speaking in powerful affirmations. Such future-based, "generative language" not only shapes your view of the future, but it also shapes your Future You. Start listening to the language you use. Your language shapes your identity, which shapes your behavior and actions, which shape your future.

Benjamin Hardy, PhD
Organizational Psychologist and Keynote Speaker
Best-Selling Author of several books,
including *Be Your Future Self Now*
He is also a dedicated husband and father of six children

ABOUT DAN MCCORMICK

DAN McCORMICK is a distinguished author, professional keynote speaker, and executive leadership teacher and coach. With an unwavering passion for the journey of self-help and the transformative power of I Am affirmations, Dan has made a significant impact in the realm of personal and professional development.

As the co-author of *Awakening Who I Am: Two Words that Ignite Your Transformation*, Dan has inspired countless individuals to embrace their true potential. His teachings emphasize the importance of affirmations, principles, habits, and reference points, providing a roadmap for lasting change.

For more than twenty-three consecutive years, Dan has dedicated himself to educating and empowering mission-driven entrepreneurs through his weekly podcast. His consistent efforts have reached thousands of individuals, helping them to generate billions in sales volume globally. Dan's insights and guidance have proven invaluable to those seeking to achieve extraordinary results in their businesses and personal lives.

Dan's book and website offer a unique combination of tools designed to facilitate immediate transformation. His practical approach and motivational style resonate deeply with audiences, making a tangible difference in their lives.

Beyond his professional achievements, Dan and his wife Marilyn are proud parents to four married daughters and grandparents to fourteen grandchildren. Dan's love for golf, yoga, and fitness, coupled with his genuine affection for people, reflects his vibrant and engaging personality. Residing in both Orange County, California, and Lake Coeur d'Alene, Idaho, Dan continues to inspire and uplift those around him with his infectious enthusiasm and profound wisdom.

For more information visit: AwakeningWhoIAm.com

ABOUT KEN SHELTON

KEN SHELTON is an expert in entrepreneurial field leadership. He served for thirty years as editor/publisher of Leadership Excellence magazines and books. Ken has been a pacesetter and visionary in the leadership development field. He has edited and published virtually every expert in the field. And he has experienced many leadership dilemmas and dramas as a business entrepreneur. He has interacted with CEOs, senior leaders, and entrepreneurs as a keynote speaker, leadership consultant, and trusted advisor. At an early age, Ken decided his life work was about becoming a leader and developing leadership in others. He has worked with and been influenced by many of the top thought leaders in the field. He is the published author of several books, including *Beyond Counterfeit Leadership: How You Can Become a More Effective Leader, Field Leadership,* and *Proactive Positivity.* He has also ghost-written dozens of bestselling books, including *Principle-Centered Leadership* and *The 7 Habits of Highly Effective People* by Stephen R. Covey.

In October 2015, Ken received the Global Leadership Excellence Award presented by the World Leadership Congress in Dubai,

Arab Emirates. He lives in Provo, Utah with his wife of fifty-two years, Mary Pamela Shelton. They are the parents of three sons and have eight grandchildren.

For more information visit: AwakeningWhoIAm.com

A SPECIAL NOTE TO ANYONE IN SALES

Dan McCormick began in the direct sales industry more than forty years ago. Over the course of his career, he has recruited and instructed thousands of sales professionals; his teams have generated in excess of a billion dollars in revenue, and created tens of millions in commissions. Dan has consistently been recognized over the years as a top leader in the field of direct sales.

Over his forty-year career, Dan has delivered speeches on thousands of stages. Today, Dan is on a mission to help individuals unlock their potential through the power of *I Am*. If you feel this message would benefit you, your sales team, or your audience at the conference you are hosting, Dan has significant expertise in educating, coaching, and instructing audiences.

If you want Dan to help you, your sales team, or your company unlock their ability to sell while transforming their personal journey, be sure to include a note about your sales experience and position when you submit an inquiry.

Reach out using any of the following methods. Include the phrase *"I Am a Magnet for Miracles"* in your submission form, or let his team know you are interested in Dan coaching or speaking with your or your team.

Email: Dan@AffirmIAm.com
Call: (949) 521-4414
Visit: www.AffirmIAm.com/Contact-Us

*BONUS OFFER

Dan takes a very small number of complimentary consultations per month. Scan this QR code to book a complimentary consultation on Dan's Calendar before all time slots fill up. We open more time slots at the beginning of each month if there are no slots available.

UNLOCKING YOUR POTENTIAL

Our mission at Affirm I Am is for you to transform your life and unlock your potential by awakening who you are. All of the power and potential of the world lies behind your ability to awaken it.

This book is the first of many. Once you have begun the journey of awakening your power, we want to guide you to ensure you finish what you start.

Take action and do not let the power and potential behind these seven phrases sit dormant on your bookshelf. Once you have felt the power of I Am and are ready to use more tools to aid you in your journey, visit our website www.AffirmIAm.com.

We have created a host of tools that will help you on your life-changing journey.

It is my mission to spread this message and help as many individuals as possible unlock their potential. In addition to the tools on my website, you can book me to speak to your team, your company, at your event, and more. I love creative collaboration, and if you have a unique idea for how I can help contribute to your journey, reach out to my team today. You can scan the QR code below or:

Email: Dan@AffirmIAm.com

Call: (949) 521-4414

Visit: www.AffirmIAm.com/Contact-Us

*BONUS OFFER

Dan takes a very small number of complimentary consultations per month. Scan this QR code to book your complimentary consultation on Dan's Calendar before all time slots fill up. We open more time slots at the beginning of each month if there are no slots available.

ABOUT DAN MCCORMICK COACHING

If you are ready to take your journey to the next level, Dan offers an exclusive one-on-one coaching program to help you develop and progress along your journey of awakening who you are. To learn more about Dan's coaching:

Email: Coaching@AffirmIAm.com
Call: (949) 521-4414
Visit: www.AffirmIAm.com/Coaching

Dan offers a limited number of complimentary consultations per month. If you are interested in speaking with Dan about his coaching program in the form of a complimentary consultation, you can book on Dan's calendar here:

AffirmIam.com

ABOUT DAN MCCORMICK
I AM RETREATS

Through Dan's forty years of business experience, he has developed exclusive connections with a variety of venues, event spaces, and retreat locations. If you are preparing to host a retreat, contact our team about what services we offer for retreats. We have a variety of options that can host small teams to a thousand individuals. Our team will coordinate all of the details. To explore these packages and offers:

Email: Retreats@AffirmIAm.com
Call: (949) 521-4414
Visit: www.AffirmIAm.com/Retreats

Dan offers a limited number of complimentary consultations per month. If you are interested in speaking with Dan about a retreat in the form of a complimentary consultation, you can book on Dan's calendar here:

AffirmIam.com

ABOUT DAN MCCORMICK ONE-ON-ONE MASTERMIND RETREATS

Finally, Dan offers a very exclusive one-on-one mastermind retreat. It is for individuals who have achieved financial success but are struggling to find greater purpose and direction in their lives. These retreats will be held at highly exclusive locations where you can coordinate anywhere from one day to an entire week with Dan. These one-on-ones will give you the chance to learn and spend an immense amount of time with Dan where he will help instruct and guide you on a variety of principles, including meditation, thought control, routine, mindset, and more.

To learn about and book your One-on-One Mastermind Retreat:

Email: Mastermind@AffirmIAm.com
Call: (949) 521-4414
Visit: www.AffirmIAm.com/mastermind-retreat

Dan offers a limited number of complimentary consultations per month. If you are interested in speaking with Dan about a One-on-One Mastermind Retreat in the form of a complimentary consultation, you can book time on Dan's calendar here:

AffirmIam.com

BOOK DAN MCCORMICK TO SPEAK AT YOUR NEXT EVENT

When it comes to choosing a professional speaker for your next event, you will find no one more respected or successful—no one who will leave your audience or colleagues with a more renewed passion for life—than Dan McCormick, one of the most gifted speakers of our generation. Since 1986, Dan McCormick has delivered more than 3,000 inspirational presentations worldwide.

Whether your audience is 10 or 10,000, and in North America or abroad, Dan McCormick can deliver a customized message of inspiration for your meeting or conference. Dan understands your audience does not want to be "taught" anything, but is rather interested in hearing stories of inspiration, achievement, and real-life people stepping into their destinies. As a result, Dan McCormick's speaking philosophy is to humor, entertain, and inspire your audience with passion and stories proven to help people achieve extraordinary results.

To schedule your complimentary, no-obligation consultation, text Dan McCormick directly with your name and your time zone at (949) 521-4414 and he will get back to you to schedule your complimentary call.

If you host an event, have a team, or hold a company retreat, Dan has spent thousands of hours on stage instructing small teams to audiences of thousands. If Dan's message of awakening who you are would resonate with your message to your audience or team, submit an inquiry to our team to get Dan on your stage:

Email: Speaking@AffirmIAm.com
Call: (949) 521-4414
Visit: www.AffirmIAm.com/Speaking

Dan offers a limited number of complimentary consultations per month. If you are interested in speaking with Dan about speaking on your stage in the form of a complimentary consultation, you can book on Dan's calendar here:

AffirmIam.com

Made in the USA
Coppell, TX
03 January 2025